Preacher's Pet

by
Amanda Jenkins Farmer

Preacher's Pet

FIRST SUNBURY PRESS EDITION
Printed in the United States of America
November 2011

Trade paperback ISBN: 978-1-934597-85-9
Mobipocket format (Kindle) ISBN: 978-1-934597-89-7
ePub format (Nook) ISBN: 978-1-934597-90-3

Published by:
Sunbury Press
Camp Hill, PA
www.sunburypress.com

Camp Hill, Pennsylvania   USA

This book is dedicated in memory of my little brother, Donnie. This is not a pleasant story about his sister and even though he's not here to read it, I know he sees every word and has given me the strength and courage to tell my story.
And to my loving husband who has stood by me through thick and thin and who was the one to tell me that I should write a book.

Foreword

Several years ago I met a certain preacher, the very one identified in this book. From the beginning, I suspected that he was what the Bible described as a wolf in sheep's clothing. My suspicions were such that I would describe them as intuition or better yet a gut reaction. Rather than projecting an aura of holiness, he reeked of filth, deception, and evil.

Being a law enforcement officer, now retired, I had often felt that sense of uneasiness around certain people. This level of discernment would guide me throughout my thirty-four year career. When I would encounter this man I felt the presence of sin emulating from a vessel of deception. It was a vivid portrait of good versus evil. The epitome of how Satan would effectively use someone to perpetrate evil by preying on the most innocent and vulnerable within our communities, our children.

One difficult part of this association was that one of my sisters was heavily involved in this preacher's ministry. Many times I tried to warn my sister of who I thought this man really was, an imposter of the Gospel. My efforts were in vain due to the fact that she loved and respected him. He knew this all too well. He used his power and control to increase that divide between my sister and I by pretending to be a victim of philosophical differences. To solidify his position of deceit he would often encourage her to pray for me. Little did I know the depth of his depraved mind.

As the years unfolded, I had the honor to be part of a child abuse team. I worked closely with social services and the Commonwealth Attorney's office. This multidisciplinary team approach allowed me to not only study but to identify certain predators. My training and experience as a criminal investigator would later confirm who I thought this man really was.

Offenders often methodically take advantage of their victims by way of ruse, domination, power, control and manipulation. The offender can be a parent, a neighbor, a step parent, a teacher, a scout leader, a coach and yes, even a preacher. These predators know exactly who their potential victims are and just how they are going to accomplish their premeditated acts of sexual abuse.

I have great admiration and respect for the victims who come forth to reveal these savage and despicable acts. These victims often step forth with simple courage and with little or no support.

So what level of motivation would drive anyone to expose such devastating and embarrassing acts? Only the victim can accurately reveal that certain drive that would lead them to step out to disclose such horrific acts of sexual abuse. I believe that the author of this book has effectively defined her motivation.

These types of crimes destroy families, communities, and innocent lives. The only feasible explanation to describe why these crimes occur is to remember who the enemy is. The bible warns us in 2 Corinthians 11: 14-15, of this, "And no wonder, for Satan himself masquerades as an angel of light. It is not surprising then, if his servants also masquerade as servants of righteousness." This description accurately describes this predator.

A motive for these types of attacks can be found in 2 Timothy 3:1-9. "There will be terrible times in the last days. 2 People will be lovers of themselves, lovers of money, boastful, proud, abusive, disobedient to their parents, ungrateful, unholy, 3 without love, unforgiving, slanderous, without self-control, brutal, not lovers of the good, 4 treacherous, rash, conceited, lovers of pleasure rather than lovers of God— 5 having a form of godliness but denying its power. Have nothing to do with such people. They are men of depraved minds, who, as far as the faith is concerned, are rejected. 9 But they will not get very far because, as in the case of those men, their folly will be clear to everyone."

The perpetrator as described in this book tried to run from his sins and from God's wrath. I cannot speak with any authority as to the depth of this man's torment. I do know that this man has felt the effects of his sins. While he may never face his crimes in open court, his judgment will be far worse. The end of verse 15 of 2 Corinthians reveals "his end will be what his actions deserve." With this promise one may find comfort rather than vengeance.

In closing I wanted to say that the storm which developed between my sister and I soon came to pass. I commend her for accepting the truth. I love her dearly and I look forward to spending eternity with her. I applaud the author for her courage and for her commitment to reveal these horrible attacks. Her desire to share this story is a tribute to her strength and determination. May she always remember that no blame ever lies with the victim.

I extend a heartfelt "Thank You," for allowing me to be part of your story. May God richly bless you and your family.

Vic Ingram, Captain (Retired)
Pittsylvania County Sheriff's Office

Introduction

It is my hope that telling my story will be of some help to someone out there; that all who read will realize that there are people all around us in positions of authority and leadership and there are so many ways for these leaders to abuse power. No matter what kind of power that it is or how good and decent those people seem to be. It can be power over just a small group of people or a tremendous amount of people. It can be the power of our teachers, our preachers, or our mentors.

Parents need to know how to protect their children from not only physical abuse but psychological as well. We as parents need to keep our eyes opened. No matter how mature or trustworthy our children are, even in the teen years, we are still their protectors and we need to make sure those in our lives know that we take that seriously.

For anyone out there who has suffered from some type of abuse, know that you are not alone. I am not a doctor but I am a survivor of it. I hope that someone can gain a little wisdom from my experience and this book. Also, see that it's okay to tell someone, talk about it and get whatever kind of help that you may need. I hope that it can help you come to the realization that you can find a way to get out of a relationship that is not right morally, according to the law or that is hurtful to you. Also, realize that you can overcome the bad memories, enjoy your life, and have peace.

Chapter One

"Welcome to our Church"

It all started one warm and sunny Saturday morning. There was a ring of the doorbell at my grandmother's home. My grandmother answered, two ladies said, "Hello, we are here to invite you to our church." My grandmother took their pamphlet and said, "Thank you." She hadn't been attending church anywhere, so she decided to attend. She went the following Sunday.

The church was a modest looking brick building with a huge grassy parking area on the side. Lined up in the lot were several school buses and vans that had the name of the church painted on the sides. My grandmother went inside. Everyone was so kind and inviting. She had enjoyed the choir singing and the Pastor's sermon.

My grandmother thought the Pastor to be a handsome, middle-aged man. He was very muscular and smooth talking with a very kind, inviting smile. He started this church about five years prior to my grandmother's visit. She fell in love with the quaint, cozy church and soon became a member.

After becoming a member of the church, she became very active. She volunteered to be a Sunday school teacher, gave money, helped with children's activities, and went door to door on Saturdays to bring people to Jesus. She was a very hard working lady, and she was very passionate about the good work that she was doing. She helped keep God's house clean and became a loyal follower of this preacher. She loved him and the members of this church. They became like a second family to her.

Not long after that, when I was eight years old, my family and I moved from our home in North Carolina. We moved back to my mother's hometown. This was where my grandmother was a member of this church.

5

My brother, sister and I were happy to live near Grandma and Papa again. I was a blonde-haired, green-eyed, timid, and quiet girl. The apple of my Papa's eye as my grandma would say. My brother was six and favored me, with blonde-hair and blue eyes. My sister was only three. On many weekends my brother, sister and I would sleep over at my grandparent's house. On Sunday mornings all of us, except Papa, would get dressed up and go to church.

We all enjoyed the classes and services. My sister was the center of attention. Everyone loved her cute round face layered with a bob type haircut. She would go in the nursery, and my little brother and I would go to children's church.

I cherished the time with my grandmother, and I saw how absorbed she was in this church. She took us to summer bible school and kids Friday fun nights. I had been to churches before so this was nothing new to me. My grandmother and my mother thought it was the best, safest place we could spend our time. However, my papa and Daddy did have their doubts about this so called man of God who was leading his flock in the direction that was "God's will."

I remember comments my papa would make and how he claimed that he would never step foot in that church. I always wondered why he felt this way. Even still, this Preacher had won over my grandma and the sixty plus members of his church, and there was almost no standing in between them. Some members of the congregation claimed they would take a bullet for their preacher. Members treated the preacher almost as if he were a "god" who could do no wrong, and who they would do anything to serve. The church ran buses to bring the children to Jesus, had vacation bible school and fun activities, all for the children. It all seemed wonderful from the outside looking in.

I loved the church from the first day I started going. I would attend every service and activity with Grandma. When she was there, I was right there with her, even when cleaning and working. I grew to look up to the Preacher like he was a second grandpa. He and his wife were very special to me. They even once took me on an all day trip to the mountains with them. I loved them both very much.

From the time I was eight years old, I was being molded. Maybe not by the Preacher necessarily, but molded just the same. I looked at this man of God like he was just that, a man of God. I knew my grandmother and many others looked up to him, trusted him, and loved him. So I did too. Less than a year after moving back to my mother's hometown, my sweet papa whom I loved dearly and was very close to suffered a severe heart attack that put him in the hospital.

He was such a good grandpa. I remember he slept on the couch when I spent nights at my grandparents' home, and I would sleep in the bed with my grandma. Sometimes he would peek in the door after Grandma was asleep while I was watching cartoons and say, "I'm going to have some ice cream would you like some?" We would go on walks around the block together and have tea parties.

He was a very special part of my life. After his heart attack, he was in the hospital a few days. I remember going to visit him and telling him that I loved him. He never got to come home from the hospital. He passed away after being there less than a week. I was devastated. I loved my papa dearly.

The Preacher preached my papa's funeral. All I remember about that day is us sitting by the graveside. My mom was holding my sister and I was beside my brother. The Preacher was standing there with all his loving words, and I remember he looked at my mom and said, "Sis, he loved you so much." And then my mom began to sob. He had all the right words during and after the service. He was always there for our family. He was seemingly a very benevolent man who loved all of the members of his church. My papa's death made the Preacher the only man in my Grandmother's life and the only grandpa in mine.

My papa's death made me a prime target. I was a target because I was so involved in church, always there and always helping out. And my parents didn't attend. My father and I didn't have a super close relationship. Everyone knows that a little girl needs that kind, loving male figure in her life. Mine was my papa, and he was now gone. This made me the perfect prey. Yes, only eight years old but still being shaped and molded to be the Preacher's pet.

The Preacher was very devoted to his members and to doing good and kind things for them. He and his wife always came to my birthday parties. They came to dinners that my grandma would have. The Preacher would socialize with my parents and family at these gatherings. He would of course invite my parents to attend church at times. Everyone got along pretty well. My daddy was an auto body mechanic, and he even painted one of the church vans at no cost to the church except for the cost of materials. Daddy was pleased to do it.

The Preacher was very loyal. His members depended on him and he was always there to visit the sick or the shut-ins or for anything a member called him for. My great-grandmother, my grandmother's mama, passed away two years after my papa, and the Preacher traveled many miles to be there for her funeral and burial. In my grandmother's eyes and so many others he was such a wonderful man. Years in the future, we learned he had motives for everything that he did. He had something to gain, and in these years he was only laying his foundation.

The Preacher would always have his office door open after services. He would let the children come in to pick a piece of candy out of his candy barrel. The kids would get their candy and often a hug from the Preacher. The church workers would pass out candy and invite children to ride the bus to church and many were brought to Christ.

The years passed by. I stayed in church and never missed a service. I was twelve years old now. For the most part I felt that I was an average preteen. I was still a blonde-haired, green-eyed girl. Only now I was very self-conscious (as most preteens are). Some would say I was pretty and mature for my age.

The church secretary had a baby when I was twelve years old. I was perfect to be a summer babysitter to help at the church with the baby while the secretary got her work done. She asked me if I would like to do this and I said that I would. Everyday she picked me up and took me back home when her work day was over.

Around this same time all the bitterness of losing my grandpa at such a young age was coming to the surface. I missed him very much. I was also confused that my parents didn't attend church. We were taught at church that not attending and living the way my parents lived was against God's will.

I was struggling with all these feelings and it hit me: if we had a problem we were supposed to go to the Preacher for help and advice. That was the biggest mistake of my life. I knocked on the Preacher's door frame because his door was always open unless someone was in there with him. He lit up and said, "Hey Manda, come in, have a seat."

I walked in and sat down. In his office, there was a big mural of a wooded area with a stream that covered the whole left wall. The windows were boarded from the outside and there were blinds with green curtains over them. The office was dimly lit by two floor-standing lamps in the corners. He had a very large desk in front of the windows and two chairs set to the side of his desk. The Preacher looked at me and smiled and asked, "What's on your mind?"

I told him that I really missed my grandpa and that I was sad that my parents didn't come to church. I don't recall receiving any kind of helpful advice, only his questions and understanding nods and looks. He had now learned just how badly I missed my grandfather and how I was confused about my home life. I remember crying and him trying to comfort me.

My parents were great parents. My daddy drank heavily at night, but he always worked and we were always provided for. I just had been taught from the Preacher and teachers at church that this was wrong and that everyone who claimed to be Christian should attend church. The Preacher knew how much my guardian at church (my grandmother) adored him. This and what I had told him was all he needed to know.

All during the summer I was there everyday of the week. Monday through Friday I was there with the secretary. Saturday I was there for church soul winning (this was going door to door inviting and finding new converts) and then Sunday morning, Sunday night and Wednesday night for church services.

On occasion while I was there during the week to babysit, the secretary would go out to run errands while her baby was napping. I would just stay there with him to keep an eye on him. One day the Preacher came out of his office and told me that he had just gotten a new game for his computer in his office and asked me if I would like to see it. I said that I would.

He sat down in his chair and I stood very closely behind and watched him play. I do remember feeling a strong connection to him. After all at this point I had known him and loved him for four years. I do believe I wanted his love and affection, and I did enjoy being with him and near him. After a few minutes he said, "Here you can sit on my lap if you'd like." I said, "Okay" and sat on his knee. A little while later we heard the secretary walk in the back door. I got up and walked out to see her.

I walked out feeling kind of happy. A little closer to a man I looked at as a grandfather figure. And I soon learned that sitting on "Grandpa's" knee wasn't enough for him.

Whenever the secretary would go out on errands, he would call me back to his office. There was small talk and joking, all done by him. I was very shy and very quiet. He soon started asking if he could give me a hug after these talks. I obliged. It felt very nice. With every hug it led more and more to holding than just hugging. That still felt good and I felt safe in his arms. At the time I never felt as though I were in the arms of a monster.

Chapter Two

"Stolen Innocence"

With summer over, the Preacher told me to come see him before church services since I was no longer there during the day. My grandmother and I always got to church a little early. I'd walk by his office which was in the same hallway as the restrooms and he would call me in to see him. Many times I would knock on the door on my own to see him. He would talk to me and was always very kind. He would ask about school, about home, and how I was. Before leaving he would have to have his hug. I always expected it and even looked forward to it. I did love the attention he gave me.

School had started. I was now in the seventh grade. I hated school and I missed being at church everyday like I had been throughout the summer. I still struggled emotionally with the death of my papa. My parents were busy. They both worked full time jobs and took care of children and a home.

I recall writing letters to the Preacher and telling him about things. He was a person I confided in about life and feelings I had about things around me. He said I could call him Grandpa, so the letters always started with "Dear Grandpa". One morning out of the blue, I decided that I wanted to run away from home. Thinking back, I don't know why, really. I don't think I knew then, maybe for attention from my parents and maybe even the Preacher. We always caught the school bus at my grandma's house and this particular morning I put water in my book bag and left a note on my grandma's bathroom mirror that I had run away. I remember thinking; I should leave a note and let her know so she won't worry that someone may have taken me.

11

I had no idea or plan of where I was going. I just snuck away when Grandma was busy and started walking. My grandmother's home was only five or six blocks from the church and that's exactly where I was drawn. I got there and was hiding in a shed behind the church. It was cold, so I decided to get on one of the buses. Maybe an hour passed. I had seen the Preacher and the secretary's cars were in the parking lot. I was sitting in the bus and a little while later I saw the Preacher walking through the lot to where the buses were.

I remember being glad to see him, but I knew someone must have called the church and I was going to be in big trouble if he saw me. I raced to the back of the bus in the hopes he wouldn't see me. He did. He walked to the back and said, "Hey Manda." I vaguely remember what all was said. He asked what was going on. I didn't say much. He talked and asked questions. I do recall him mentioning after a while of talking that he had never seen me in jeans before (for church we girls always wore skirts or dresses and this was a school day, so I had on a pair of jeans). He told me to come to him. He hugged me for a few minutes and then said that we needed to call my parents.

I was indeed in trouble for scaring everyone. I promised that I would never do anything like that again. I remember being asked why I did it, and I just told them I didn't know. My daddy was very angry and told me that the Preacher had asked about me staying with him and his wife for a few weeks. I think maybe Daddy was offended by that and knew I would possibly enjoy it too much. When he said that, I did wish that he would let me. He looked me in the eyes and said, "That is not happening young lady. What I would like is to turn you over my knee, but for now you go pull the weeds out of the garden!!"

I love my daddy. He taught us to be decent, good people, and hard workers. At the time, however, I wasn't too thrilled. I pulled the weeds and there was a little tension for the next few days but we moved passed it and things got back to normal.

The Easter Sunday, a few months after my thirteenth birthday, the church was going to have a sunrise service outside of a member's home. After the service was over I smiled and walked over to stand beside the Preacher. He nervously walked away. I knew something was wrong because normally he would talk for a minute even in front of others. Something had changed but I couldn't imagine what. Back at church, I tapped on his door. He said, "Come in."

The room smelled of cologne. He was sitting behind his desk and looked up at me over his glasses. I stood there as he talked for a moment. He stood up, walked over in front of me and took me by the hands. Still holding my hands, he sat down in the chair in front of me. He looked as though he were very tired and drained for some reason. He placed his hands on my hips and took a deep breath and said to me, "Amanda, when I hug you it makes me want to do other things."

I'm sure that I had a puzzled look on my face. He said, "It makes me want to touch you." He still could see my confusion. He said, "It makes me want to touch you here", as he ran his hand across the front of my skirt. He paused for a minute and asked, "Would you tell anyone?" I looked around. I thought for a moment, and said, "No, I won't." He already knew that or he would not have asked.

He smiled, seemed very relieved and stood up. He then asked if he could kiss me on my lips. He instructed me to open my mouth a little and proceeded to teach me how to french kiss. I was only thirteen. I had never even held a boy's hand, much less kissed one. For most girls, a first kiss is very special. For me it was wrong and dirty.

When I walked out for a second I thought, Ew! But other than that, I think I was flattered. I was flattered, and thought I'm his favorite, I'm special to him. This great man of God wants me? This was rather exciting for me. I had been instructed to keep this secret from my family, my friends, and the Preacher's wife. She was a very beautiful, well shaped brunette and my beloved Sunday school teacher and mentor. I recall this particular church service, after he had confessed to me his feelings and taught me how to kiss him that he seemed very bubbly and happy. So much so, that I even thought to myself, I think I did that. I made him happy.

13

By the next service we were talking again and he asked me had I gotten my period yet. I thought this to be an odd, personal question, but I told him I had. He mentioned how attracted to me he was when he saw me a few months before on the church bus wearing jeans. He told me that I looked so good in them. I also found this to be strange, I think because I couldn't wrap my mind around that. I couldn't wrap my mind around it, because it was not normal.

In one of our meetings after touching and kissing me wherever he pleased, he would have his version of pillow talk. He mentioned something about when we used to only hug, how when I would drop my arms, my hands would run across his private area, accidentally. He smiled and said, "You liked that didn't you?" I just smiled at him. I had no idea that my hands did that, and I certainly wasn't in the place where "I liked it." He gave me that look and said that he liked it.

In our closed-door sessions, he began confiding in me about his marriage, his family, and his two grown children. How his son had been arrested for pimping in California, his son-in-law's gambling and pornography addictions. All the while he was telling me that he had fallen madly in love with me and that he desperately needed me. This was a lot for a thirteen year old to take in.

He would tell me constantly that he never meant for this to happen and that I was the ONLY other woman other than his wife. I was old enough to know what was going on with us and that we were in fact in a relationship. He had told me that the love he felt for me was the love a man feels for a woman. I thought and believed that I had that same kind of love for him. He would beg that even after he was dead to never tell a soul. He said that I was born in the wrong time and that I should have been with him, and how he wished I were older. I did love hearing that I was the most beautiful "woman" in the church and that he loved me so much.

He told me that his dear, loving wife would probably commit suicide if she ever found out about our relationship. He always made sure that I knew how severe the consequences would be if anyone found out. I was so infatuated with everything about him that I believed all this. Not that I would have told anyway. I believed that God had brought us together and we were in love and that he needed me, and I needed him, just like he had always told me. In reality, God was nowhere near that office or that relationship.

There was once an incident at church when I was there babysitting on Spring break while the secretary's child was napping. As you walk in the side door of the church, there is a hall and to the left was a room and through that room was the secretary's office. When you go straight down the hall you would come to a corner. When you turn the corner, the hall led to where the Preacher's office was.

That particular day I was doing something in the room beside the secretary's office. He was in his office, and he knew the secretary had left. He came out of his office to see me.

He said, "We'll stay here that way when the secretary pulls in the parking lot we'll hear her." We were kissing and all of a sudden we heard her coming in the door. He quickly backed away and acted as though he had stepped out of his office to get something. She looked at us and had a strange look on her face as though she thought something didn't seem right. I was trying my best, but I know I must have looked guilty. Nothing was said about that at the time.

Here I was the Preacher's plaything, but in my mind I was more. He made me believe I was. I would listen in the church pews as he would preach against sin and wrongdoing. He would preach how we should live a just life. All the while he was taking his time and planning out how he would continue to have his way with a young girl every chance he could.

At the time I didn't think he was doing anything wrong with me. He told me over and over that our situation was an exception. He had taught me that this was a special circumstance. Like the rules didn't apply to him or us. I was a very misguided girl. I was misguided and manipulated by a person who was supposed to be setting an example for his church and living a life for God.

Although this man was only human, he was a man who God held to a higher standard because of his position.

During my thirteenth year there was a lot of kissing that led to more fondling and touching. He would press his body against mine. He would ask me to touch him. At first this made me uncomfortable, but at the same time I was a teenager with hormones. I was also a teenager with a lot of emotional issues because of this confusing relationship. I felt I was in love and would do any and everything that he asked, and I did, with no question and no hesitation. I strove to please him no matter what.

I know he planned it that way. He knew I was fully and completely his, all by looking in my eyes. He had a way of looking at me like he could see right through me. He knew exactly how vulnerable I was and he used that to his advantage. He knew exactly how to bring me to my knees and to make me desperate for more time with him.

I would find ways to have my grandmother leave me at church. I told her I had some project to work on or something that I needed to do for someone. And she would leave me, mainly on Sunday mornings after church, because she would be back for the evening service, even if the Preacher was there in his office. She was confident that I was safe there and she probably felt I was even safer when he was there.

Behind closed doors, before church services all this brainwashing and abuse of power was taking place. All the while his congregation was out waiting for him to deliver one of his powerful Godly messages. All the while his wife was out there waiting to hear her husband. The piano player was playing hymns and the choir was getting ready to make a joyful noise unto the Lord. Everyone was waiting to hear a man they loved. Unbeknownst to them they were waiting to hear a sexual predator speak his opinion about a God he knew nothing of.

Chapter Three

"The Christian School"

The Preacher always claimed that a dream of his was to run a Christian school. Plans for this school came to pass. I remember well the night the church had the meeting to talk about it and how excited I was. The Preacher had looked into hiring an assistant pastor who could run the school and take care of things. This assistant pastor came and brought his family. They were very sweet, well-meaning people who I believe wanted to serve God. They got to work to get our Christian school up and running. My parents couldn't afford the tuition, but that was no problem. The Preacher had to be sure his play thing was there everyday of the week, always there at his beck and call.

I was excited about this because I felt I belonged at this school. I never liked school, really, but I felt this school would be different. It was a small group of students and I did enjoy going there and being with my friends. I was so shy that I was never comfortable in public school with a lot of the teachers and students. I knew that I would like this small private school so much better.

Now, instead of sitting in class at public school daydreaming about the man I loved, I could see him everyday. I was thrilled by this idea. By this time my brother had lost interest in the church and was no longer attending, and my sister would be a part of the school the next year.

Everyone worked hard to get things ready. Some men at church built school desks for the school. The Preacher's wife and I stained the desks. The day the two of us were there working, the Preacher was there. His wife and I were sitting side by side and he said, "Say cheese!" And he snapped a picture of us.

Everything was ready and the first year was well off to a start. The Preacher interacted with all of the students just like a regular person would. He knew all of them and their parents from church. He would joke and talk with the teachers and students on a daily basis. To me and to everyone he seemed to be a normal and good man who would never do the things that he did. He was very smart and careful. He also knew he had enough people that loved him and trusted him so much that they would NEVER question him. He used all of this to his advantage.

The school was very small. It only consisted of two to three teachers at a time and at the most twenty students at a time. The Preacher came every day and would go study in his office. He would go home for lunch and would on most days even come back after lunch. On our class lunch breaks or our short fifteen-minute breaks, the Preacher would see me walk by his door and have me come in for a few minutes for his pleasure. Usually this was kissing and necking. Whenever I had on a button up top, he would unbutton it and fondle and suck my breasts.

He asked me once if I ever masturbated. I was so thrown by the question, I said nothing for a minute and he started to tell me what it meant. I quickly interrupted and said, "I know what it means!" He laughed and said, "Okay." I said, "No, I don't. That's weird." I did know what it meant; I had been in public school around kids who talked about things like that. He then said, "Well you should try doing it and think of me." I suppose he realized that he would do things to me, and always leave me unsatisfied, all the while pushing me out the door for fear too much time had passed.

On the school day meetings he knew no one would notice that I was in the Preacher's office, AGAIN. I believe now he liked the thrill of sneaking around with someone and knowing that he was getting away with something. He would have me perform oral sex, which had happened before, but more often after the school started. The first time was one homecoming Sunday, or a Sunday that we

had dinner after the morning church service. I remember
he had gradually talked the act up to me.

This particular Sunday after the dinner, some people
had left already, and some of the ladies were cleaning up. I
remember I was sitting at a table and I looked up and saw
him in the fellowship hall doorway. He gave me a look that
I responded to like a robot. I knew it meant to follow him to
his office. When I walked in, he locked the door behind
me. He asked me if I would do what he had talked about.
I shook my head. He unzipped his pants and sat down in
the chair beside his desk and I got on my knees. I found
this to be extremely disgusting, but I never let him know. I
wanted to make him happy, so no matter what he asked,
whenever he asked, I was his. Right then he had me
exactly where he wanted me.

One day he called me out of class. When we walked in
his office he grabbed me and started to kiss me. He would
often hold my face in his hands and look into my eyes, run
his fingers over my eyes, cheeks and lips and say, "You are
so beautiful, so sweet, and so innocent." Then he would
hold me and say, "I love you so much! Amanda, you are so
special to me." He always made sure I felt special. I did
feel special and loved. He had a way of being so loving,
gentle and affectionate, things that so many women crave
in a relationship. He knew well what he was doing and
how to do it. I always felt his wife was so blessed to have
him.

Another instance, I was in with him and we were
talking. He looked at me and said, "You looked just like
your mama when you made that face. God, they would kill
me if they knew!" He knew I would never tell them because
I loved him too much. He could see it all over the face that
looked "so much like my mama's."

He would have these days when he was so serious. He
would look me in the eyes so intensely that I would often
have to look away. I was very bashful and it was so hard
to just stare into his eyes that way. When I looked away,
he would take my face in his hands and turn my eyes back
toward his. It was like he could just stand with me for
hours just holding and stroking my hands and looking into
my eyes. He would say, "I need you, Amanda". Usually, I

would say, "You've got me". He knew he had me. He then would grab me and hold me. It felt good to be "needed".

After the school started I was there everyday. There in the house of God where Godliness was a joke. The Preacher's wife and I were very close. She was a good teacher and would host activities and sleepovers with her teenage girl's class. Once we had a sleepover at their home. The bed in the spare bedroom was full of girls, so I was the one who slept on the couch.

The Preacher was supposed to get up early to go hunting the next morning. I heard his footsteps in the kitchen, but stayed facing the opposite direction. A part of me wanted to turn around, but I didn't. When I saw him at church the next day he had mentioned to me something about him getting up so early the morning before. I told him I knew and that I had slept on the couch and heard him. He told me had he known it was me on the couch he would have come over to see me.

I was getting a little wiser now, and I did truly love his wife. I thought to myself, Really? With your wife in the other room, who could walk in anytime? I never said a word until one day I came to realize something must be wrong in their relationship. We were talking and I thought maybe I could help him "fix" their marriage. "What's wrong with you and your wife?" I asked. In my mind, I thought, she's beautiful, she's thin, and she seems so wonderful, so what's the deal? He looked at me strangely and said, "Nothing" kind of angrily.

He said, "My wife is very affectionate." I replied, "Well why don't you just go home and hold her, and love her?" (I said this in a loving manner and felt that I wanted to help) He then said, "Well she's different since our daughter moved away." He paused and said, "All I know is that I love you more than anyone in this world". I thought to myself, more than anyone in this world? Wow!

And that was that. I was apparently his number one girl. I accepted those answers and nothing changed. While he had me where he wanted me, over the clouds in love, he was talking to his secretary and maybe his wife telling them that I had problems and that I was a very troubled girl. He told them that someone must have abused or molested me as a young child.

I found this out years later and came to realize that it was more of his groundwork. He was covering his tracks in case I ever told anyone about us. That way he would have witnesses to claim that he had told them all along that I was crazy. It would then be my word against his. All this and then some was going on behind the curtain of my life. Many years later I found out that he was not only lying to me but he was also lying about me.

Chapter Four

"The Other Woman"

There were always very deep conversations between the Preacher and myself. Conversations in which he would even say, "I'm sorry I've done this. I just fell in love with you. I need you and you need me. Don't you?" At times it was like I had to assure him that I did need him and want him. And that what he was doing to me was okay. I felt I did need him. I felt that he was the best thing that had ever happened to me. He always knew the right things to say. During those years I thought it was because his feelings were genuine and that he truly loved me.

He would also admit that what he was doing was wrong and he knew it. He said on several occasions, "God is going to kill me." This was usually after whatever he wanted was done and sometimes when we were only talking. It was almost as if he was remorseful. This made me feel horrible, like I was the reason he was doing wrong. However, no matter how bad or sorry I would feel sometimes, it seemed to be worth it for me, and for him.

I recall being in his office one day and he looked at me and said, "Amanda I want you to know that I never thought in a million years that something like this would happen between me and any woman besides my wife. There has never, never, never, been any woman other than my wife." He said all this with much enthusiasm as he was shaking his head and gesturing with his hands. He was very convincing. Little did I know I wasn't the only one he was saying these things to. Now I know he was telling that lie so loud and so often in the hopes of maybe making himself believe it.

I loved his wife very much. I never thought of my relationship with her husband as something against her. I think I wouldn't allow my mind to think that way, or to think how devastated she would be had she found out. I wasn't stupid. I was young, but I was not ignorant. I knew what was happening, but the Preacher had me believe our relationship was unusual, yes, but something unique and alright, because we loved each other so deeply.

As I grew and matured, I suppose the Preacher wanted more. For whatever reason, we would be at church alone more often. He would talk about sex and tell me how much he wanted it with me. He would then say that it was such a small part of life and once we did it, we would want to everyday. He said that we would have sex when the time was right. I would just smile and say okay. He knew I was very easily persuaded and would go along with whatever he said.

Then one day sort of unplanned he had me come in his office. He told me to go to the bathroom, remove my panties from underneath my skirt and then come back. This made me very nervous, but I did as he instructed. When I walked back into the office and closed the door behind me, he walked over and carefully locked the door. He whispered for me to hold onto the arms of the chair and bend over. He then pulled up my skirt.

This was not the special first time girls in a normal relationship plan for. It was also not what I had been taught in church from behind the pulpit. I was not a grown, married woman. At the time I was not thinking about these things. I only thought about pleasing him no matter how uncomfortable or embarrassing it was for me. I loved him and realized this was something he desired, and even though it made me very self conscious, I went along with what he wanted.

I assumed him having me lean over the chair was safer in case someone were to come in the church, than if we were unclothed and on the floor. What he was doing did hurt me a little, but I said nothing. After a few minutes of him trying to penetrate he pulled away and had his handkerchief. He smiled and simply said, "Too much foreplay." He proceeded to zip his pants and then he hugged me for a minute and said, "I guess we should open the door."

This was the first time he attempted intercourse. I was fourteen. It was times like these or when he was holding me before a service and someone would knock on the door and he would almost push me down, to get me away for fear of being caught, that I felt used and uncared for. I brushed these feelings aside, and it was overlooked until the next time.

He would never ask me to perform oral sex or try anything more than a kiss or a hug before a church service most of the time. He would always insinuate that it would hinder the church service and God working. Also, there were more people there and a good chance that someone would knock on his door or need to see him.

Again, this made me feel that he tried to do right as far as his preaching and his church, but at times he just couldn't control himself. I felt he was making a sacrifice because he loved me. A sacrifice because he did feel bad, but he loved me, so it was worth feeling bad to have me. All this would go through my mind: our forty year age difference and how totally wrong that aspect of it was. However, it wasn't that much of an issue for me at that time.

I knew he was old enough to be my grandfather and deep down I knew how sick it really was but it did not matter to me, really. I was attracted to him. He was much older, but he was in the category of men who get more attractive with age. He was very handsome and distinguished. He knew it. He was also very cocky. And maybe I didn't allow myself to really evaluate our situation. Love was blind. I suppose as my grandma always said, "Love was deaf, dumb and blind." I loved with my whole heart, unconditionally. He knew that and he used me and he felt completely safe doing it. He took total advantage of my love, a love that when it began, for me was totally innocent. He made my love into something it should have never been.

He attempted intercourse another day that we were at church alone. This time he had me lie on the floor (still fully clothed aside from my panties). As I laid there nervous and uncomfortable he straddled me and stared at me and said, "You are the sexiest woman I have ever seen."

He lifted my skirt and attempted, and didn't stop until he was finished, though he did not completely penetrate.

The next time we were alone he had me stand while he was on his knees. My arms were around his neck, his hands were up my skirt as he crammed some kind of plastic cylinder object inside me in the hopes that the next time he could make it happen. He explained to me why he had to do this.

In my young mind I thought I wanted this to happen, even though it was all so strange to me. I thought I wanted this with him. Therefore, I would go to the same extremes that he did to keep this relationship a secret. I never knew or thought about how fifteen plus years later it would still be affecting my life in a bad way and probably in some way will as long as I live.

I got strep throat once as a teenager, and I was terrified to go to the doctor. I was afraid that something was wrong with my throat because of what I had been doing. I would have rather died than us be found out. I called him at church before my mama took me to the doctor and asked could there be something wrong with me because of that. He laughed and told me no. I trusted him fully, so I was relieved.

Even if I would have had someone ask me was there something happening with us, I would have lied. I would have done all I could to keep this secret. He never forced me to do anything, so to me it was all okay. I felt as though I was old enough to know what I wanted and I thought I wanted all the same things that he did. By that, I mean to be together and to be in a relationship in which everything else comes after "love," including sex.

All these years later I now know that we didn't want the same things. I wanted love and a relationship, (that's what he tricked me into believing he could give me, when in "real life" of course he could not) and he wanted my virginity. I also realize now that I was not old enough to know what I wanted and that I was solely basing my choices on his powerful influence. I now see that deep down on the inside of the preacher is a devil, a selfish man, who only wanted to gratify himself. It mattered not that he was ruining that time of my life in the process. He projected to his church a nice man full of goodness and love. He kept his true self hidden very well.

Luckily, the opportunities for him to attempt intercourse were few and far between. He knew it was far too dangerous when people were there (and even when no one was there, but could come in the church at any time) and he was always careful. I say he was always careful, but there were many times he would just lock the door and risk it, believing in the trust that all the people had in him. He knew no one would ever suspect any wrongdoing on his part. Some of them were so blind that they wouldn't believe it, even if they walked right in on it.

The following winter there was going to be a trip to Indiana to a Christian conference. All the teenagers were urged to go. We took the church van and the Preacher drove his vehicle. A friend and I rode with him and his wife on this fifteen-hour trip. He would make eyes at me in the rearview mirror. As we were getting in and out of the car, in between other cars in the dark he would sexually rub against me as he walked by.

I enjoyed all of this attention. I still remember being envious of his wife and wishing I could be her. I was jealous of her, but not in a mean way. I wanted to switch places with her. I felt I would have given up forty years of my life to trade places with her, to be with him. Today, I am thankful that I am not her. I would not want to be a woman who had to find out that the man she has been married to for more than half of her life turned out to be someone she couldn't even recognize.

I often wonder if his wife ever suspected that her husband was not being faithful. I'm sure if she had, she would have never thought he was being unfaithful with a child. I believe he also had some type of power and control over her just as he did with so many other women. I hope that his wife was not a woman who suspected something and just turned the other cheek. I have read books and learned how many women are involved with their husband's crimes. If she had any idea and did nothing, then I believe she is just as guilty as he is. I often wonder what kind of life and marriage they had and how he lived his life in the open before he "found Jesus" and started a church. Once he became a Christian and a Preacher he would have to hide his transgressions.

I walked into the church in between meetings of this church conference after being on a lunch break. The Preacher and his wife had gotten back to their seats before the rest of us. Both of their hands were on the top of the pew and he was stroking hers. I had a sinking feeling and turned around and walked out. I guess they saw me because he later asked me about it. He said to me, "I'm sorry you had to see that."

He was apparently playing into my youth and immaturity. After all they were only holding hands. But it all hit me and I saw firsthand that they were husband and wife. Of course, I already knew that, but for some reason that day it just smacked me right in the face. It made me realize that I was the other woman. I felt the jealousy and hurt of that. It was not a good feeling. I did mention to the Preacher on several occasions that one day when I found someone for me that he would understand my jealousy and how I was feeling.

Chapter Five

"More Secrets"

The Preacher and his wife lived in a very beautiful home that the church paid for, and they both drove very nice cars. He was a car salesman as well as the pastor of the church. Rumor had it that he was involved in some fishy business as far as his car business went. There were constantly members coming and going from the church. Some left because they didn't agree with all the Preacher's opinions. I wonder now what the deeper reasons could have been. We all knew it was his way or the highway. A lot of people chose the highway.

When members would leave he would bash them from behind the pulpit and say how they were out of God's will. Some kind of drama was always going on with members. Some would leave; some would work it out and stay. But the Preacher always had his faithful followers that would follow until the end. They always said it and the Preacher knew it.

He was a very controlling man that had the need to dominate everything. He truly thought he was the shepherd and his congregation, were the sheep. He would make it clear that he called the shots and made the rules. All of his loyal followers seemed to be okay with that on the outside. He would pressure young boys into saying God was leading them to preach. I still don't understand his reasoning behind that. Maybe that was just something else he could control.

In my fifteenth year there were more attempts at intercourse. I think now they just weren't close enough together for him to completely penetrate without hurting me. In that way, I was at least being kept from being hurt. He had told me that we didn't have to worry about me getting pregnant because he had a vasectomy after his second child was born, so he never wore protection.

He was very proud of his "manhood." He would brag about his size, and how as a young adult if he had on a pair of fitting pants, his buddies would think he was "coming up," as he said they called it back then. I was not fascinated by conversations along these lines. They made me uncomfortable. We had been doing this for years, but I still was not completely at ease with him. Even if I were, I wouldn't care to talk that way.

There were more conversations along the lines of his fantasies. Would I run away with him when I turned eighteen? He spoke on several occasions how it would be after I was married. He would say, "To everyone else I'm like your grandpa so when you get married, Grandpa can live in a section of your house because you need to take care of me. When your husband goes to work you can come in my room and take care of me." As he said this, he raised his eyebrows up and down and smiled.

I think about this now and think, Wow! That is really disturbing. Of course the whole situation is. At the time I would humor him and say yes, and agree with everything that he said. Somewhat knowing it was all talk. I also knew that I wanted something normal one day, but I wondered if I could ever feel the same way about another man. Like him, I did often wish that I were his age or that he were mine and that we could officially be together. I told him that I was afraid that I would never love anyone else the way I loved him. I would wonder if this was still happening when I turned eighteen if he would ask me to run away with him.

I had thought about it and I knew that if we were to be together that we would have to run away and leave everyone behind, everyone including his children and grandchildren. I felt that I would not allow that, because I did love him. I knew if we did that, that he would maybe be happy at first, but most likely would grow to resent me because his children and so many others would hate him. So, really I was the one thinking like the grown up and he was behaving and thinking like the child.

He told me once that I should write a letter to his grandson, who was my age, and invite him to church. I had never met him. The Preacher's son and his grandson's mother were divorced. He said that maybe he would come to church and I could get to know him. He then smiled and said, "He would love you and we can keep it all in the family". I remember thinking that was a little strange. I also thought I don't want him, I want you.

As my story goes, it is now two, almost three years into this ongoing "affair." I thought I was happy with the way things were. But I slowly came to realize that I wasn't happy that I only got to spend ten to fifteen minutes at a time with the man I loved. I was hurt by that, but I knew that's how it had to be. He knew I felt this way. I told him. He told me that he felt the same way, but that we have to appreciate and enjoy any minute that we had together.

I still knew how important it was for this relationship to be kept secret. As I said, I loved his wife very much. She was always very special to me. When I was fifteen I helped plan a surprise birthday party for her. I made cupcakes and finger foods. A few of the other girls in our Sunday school class helped. We were to have her party after our Sunday night service. After the morning service I decorated and set up for the party. The choir had choir practice after the service and that's when we got the last minute things ready.

During the evening service, I began to feel really sick. I don't know if I had food poisoning or what, but I was terribly sick. While we were waiting for his wife to finish choir practice the Preacher noticed I was sick, back and forth from the restroom and he offered me some stomach medicine. I told him thank you, but I don't think it will help and that it would just come back up. He said why don't you go ahead and get your grandma to take you home. I told him about his wife's party and how I wanted to be there for it. There weren't too many people that I would wait around for, while I was so sick and should have been in bed. I loved her and I wanted to do it for her. Sometimes I wonder now if my love and devotion to her was a way of being closer to him.

After the school had been up and running a few years, the assistant pastor left, or was run off from the church. I believe he could see some of the Preacher's true colors and maybe sensed things, where all others had blinders on. He went on to become a pastor of his own church. When he left, the school was then run by the Preacher's niece who had been attending the church and working in the school.

The Preacher would feel at ease enough to walk in the school room and ask to see me whenever the mood struck. This was nothing unusual and it seemed no one thought anything of it. I was thrilled on these times, because it would mean, a little more than ten or fifteen minutes. I think he probably had everyone believing that I needed counseling. I honestly wonder now where he thought it would go and how long it could last. Also, how was he so sure that I would never tell?

One day I was in his office and he said, "Someday I'm going to take you to a hotel...rip your clothes off...take a shower with you...rub soap all over your body and finally get the chance to make love to you." He mentioned sending his wife to California to visit their daughter and somehow sneaking me to his house. I could tell he had put much thought into this fantasy. He had planned the details up to what I could tell my parents and how I could duck down in the floor of the car until he parked it in his garage and could walk me right into the house. I admit at the time all this did entice me. But I didn't care where we were or what we were doing. I just wanted time with him.

I believed that we were in love and that he was the man of my dreams. I agreed to his plans, but never thought any of them would be possible anyway because he was always, always very cautious. Even to the point of telling me over and over throughout the years to never write anything down or keep a journal.

All those years of being manipulated and taken total advantage of, I always did everything he said. I had friends, but of course I would never tell them. Even though he made me happy and I had that desire to share these feelings with my friends. I knew it would be over if I had. It has now been fifteen years and the joke is on him! I am writing things down in the hopes that the whole world reads and can be warned to beware of the possibility that men in their lives could very well be like him.

At that time in my life, I wondered if I would ever have a real boyfriend or get married. There were boys at church who I called my boyfriend at spells, but nothing real. There was a guy in my neighborhood that was crazy about me, but by the time I was old enough to have a real boyfriend, my time and thoughts were consumed by the Preacher. I thought no one else could measure up. I didn't feel I really wanted anyone else. I always felt that I would have the Preacher's love and he would have mine until the day he died. My thoughts and feelings soon changed.

Chapter Six

"Not So Sweet Sixteen"

My sixteenth birthday was approaching and I was excited like most sixteen year olds to get a job and to be able to drive. The only problem was that I had this emotional burden on my shoulders all the time. I was trying to live up to the church's (his) rules and standards for all the school students, and on top of it all, he had a plan.

He began talking more and more about meeting me at a hotel, in a town over of course, to be on the safe side. He had already stolen my first kiss, my innocence and my heart and he now wanted to be sure to take my virginity as well. Had we started meeting at hotels, it would have most definitely happened.

I said I would do it if he made the plans. I believe I was just happy at the thought of being able to just be with him without being afraid of getting caught or being pushed away. I hated the hurt that I felt when we never had enough time together. I believed a hotel room was our chance to have that time.

I celebrated my sixteenth birthday with my family. To this day, my mama throws us all a party with cake, ice cream, presents, and the works! I wished I could celebrate with the man I loved, but that was impossible. We could never really be together, though I would often fantasize about a life with him. The Preacher would always give me money on birthdays and Christmases, never an actual gift because someone may ask where I had gotten it.

I got my license and started looking for a job. I searched and searched. I even had the hopes that when I found a job that I could meet someone I could actually be seen with, sit beside and have a real relationship with. That was MY plan. It made me feel sad that the Preacher and I couldn't really be together. It had been this way for years. I was growing up and changing. I had become a little angry and tired of having to be hidden.

My grandma was still going to church. Until I got a car she would always pick my sister and me up and bring us to church. She even took me around to apply for jobs. I finally got a call for an interview at the local Harris Teeter. I was hired on the spot and went ahead with my training to be a cashier.

After I had worked for a while the Preacher wanted to help me buy a car. He was so thoughtful. Of course he had his own reasons. So he went with my mom and me to the bank and co-signed for a loan for my first car. I got the car and was now busy with school and work. I now had a license and a car so his plans were being made for a hotel room. He was just waiting for the right time. Fortunately for me, God had a different plan.

Chapter Seven

"My Angel"

One busy Saturday at work, the grocery store was swamped. I was ringing up customers. I turned to see a new, very handsome bagger walk up beside me and start bagging groceries. He had black hair, was tall and very handsome. He smiled and said, "I see you're in training." (I didn't have my uniform yet) I said, "Yes" and smiled. Even though with all I had experienced at my young age I was still very shy. He had just graduated from high school and transferred from another store.

I could tell he had a sweet soul and was a little bashful himself. Weeks went by and I would see him watching me. I had a feeling he liked me, but he never said anything.

Everything was all the same at school and church. The Preacher was still handing out his orders and the members were bowing to the master. He was spilling the beans to me as usual about things and problems members were having that they had confided in him about. He told me about problems in marriages and families. I don't know if it was his way of being close to me or just plain gossip.

A few more weeks had gone by since the new bagger started working. I realized that he (his name was Eddie) wasn't going to make the first move. So, one night I was getting off work and I walked by as he was restocking the dairy case. I told him bye and then I turned around and asked, "Would you like to come to church with me some time?" He smiled and said, "Yes." So I gave him my phone number. He called that weekend.

The Preacher and I were talking and I told him my exciting news. I had met someone at work and invited him to church. Needless to say he wasn't thrilled, but he tried to pretend to be happy for me. Deep down he had to know this was probably the beginning of the end of us. Eddie met my parents and started coming to church with me.

He would pick me up in his Camaro. We got dirty looks because it was "wrong" for teens of the opposite sex to ride alone together. That's what I'd been taught at church. I didn't care. I thought to myself, they can think what they want, and if they only really knew who they were getting their rules from.

When I first met Eddie, I still would go see the Preacher. At first I thought that would be fine. He was my secret and I thought we could live like we had always talked about. Even though I had to grow up, move on and maybe even get married, "I could still take care of Grandpa." I could really sense his anger and jealousy of Eddie, even though he tried to hide it. I was confused and that made the Preacher confused.

I was sixteen and still growing and changing. One day he was holding me and I guess my body was too close to his. He gently pushed me back like he was frustrated and said, "Amanda, I don't know what you want. You haven't been to see me much and now you come in here rubbing your body against mine. You're making me crazy!" I said, "I'm sorry!" I knew then something needed to change.

So after dating Eddie for a few weeks I stopped going in his office and soon really had no desire to go see that man that I thought I loved so much. It was like I had put a wall in between the Preacher and my mind, like he wasn't allowed there anymore. I wouldn't allow myself to want him. The really peculiar thing was he never came to get me out of class either. I could sense when speaking in passing a little resentment on his part. It hurt a little, but I didn't lose any sleep over it.

Eddie didn't know it, but he had saved me from my preacher. He had saved me from losing more of myself to him. He saved me from a man who should have been my mentor, a person I could trust, a person my friends and family and fellow church members could trust. Eddie was my angel and didn't even know it yet.

I was now close to seventeen and Eddie and I were growing closer and closer. We really cared about each other, and he was such a good guy. I felt so many times that I didn't deserve him. On a funny note, I think after a few months of dating I would finally eat in front of him. We would go on drives and to the park.

My parents really liked him and knew he was a very good guy. He was a perfect gentleman. I had let him know up front that I had every intention of saving my "first" kiss for my wedding day. After all, I had been taught this way from behind the pulpit BUT taught differently behind the office door. I was confused, but tried to be a good person and to do what was right.

I turned seventeen and Eddie had flowers sent to school for me. He would come have lunch with me at school if he got out of class in time. (He was attending a community college in town). We would also see each other at work.

At work there was a contest going on for the customers and the employees. Each customer and employee would get a game card. The cards had different prizes with a section on each prize for three game pieces. If you filled in the three sections you would win that prize.

Every time a customer would make a purchase they would receive a game piece. Every time an employee would get a paycheck they would receive a game piece. The customer game pieces and employee pieces were different to insure that no one could cheat.

It was a few weeks into the game and I hadn't really been playing, but I was keeping the pieces. I had four or five pieces saved so I decided to get a game card when I got off work and take it home. I got in my car and drove down our gravel road into the woods where our little house was. I went in and the house was filled with the smell of mama cooking supper. I sat down and ate my supper. After eating I went back to my room to open the pieces.

I opened them and much to my surprise I had all three pieces for the $20,000 prize! I ran in the kitchen to show my family and none of us could believe it. My mama was in such disbelief she said, "Something must be wrong." So my sister and I rode to Harris Teeter to see the manager. Sure enough, I had won the $20,000 prize. I walked out of there on cloud nine. We were all so happy. I went straight home to call Eddie and tell him my good news.

Now I was thinking, I can go to this Christian college that every one at church said I should go to. When I told Eddie this he wasn't too glad to hear it because it meant I would be moving away. He was very happy that I had won the grand prize at work though. Getting a job at Harris Teeter was one of the best things that ever happened to me. It brought forth riches and a great guy!

The next day at school I told everyone the news. I also went to see the Preacher to tell him. He was happy because I had to tithe ten percent to the church. I, thinking of it now, know that money probably went straight to his pocket. He stopped me later, after I received the money and asked where it was. I told him that my dad and I had put it in the bank. My daddy wanted to put some of it in the best place for it to earn interest for me.

The Preacher asked, "Is it in your name or your daddy's?" I said, "Both." He said, "Well that worries me because what if your daddy takes it? I know he wouldn't do it sober, but what if he got drunk and did it?" Deep down, I knew my daddy would never do that in any frame of mind. The Preacher said, "You should get it and put it some place else in your name only." So me being the idiot who believed him, that's what I did.

I knew by doing that, I would hurt my daddy and make him angry. The Preacher had planted that seed of doubt about my father, and it got bigger and bigger. So I thought I should move in with my grandmother to take some of the pressure off.

That's what I did. All in one afternoon while my parents were at work. I got the money and my things and I left. I ran away to my grandma's because this preacher was trying to come between my parents and me even more. As if it wasn't enough that he'd put lies and secrets between us. He wanted me to doubt who they were as well.

So I was now living with my grandmother. My parents were hurt that I just left that way, but we worked through it and decided it wasn't a bad idea for me to be with my grandmother since she was getting older. She and I were like best buddies, so it all worked out. And I think in the long run my parents and I became closer.

38

Eddie was still coming to church with me. He and I were sitting under this ungodly "Man of God" and my feelings were about to change. I still felt in my heart that the Preacher never meant for all of it to happen and that he just fell in love with me. And of course I was the only one other than his wife.

The Preacher was always friendly to me, and he would stop me to talk occasionally. He would say, "I miss you, and I still love you with all my heart." He told me that he felt jealous of Eddie and he said, "You told me one day I would know how you felt didn't you?" I simply shook my head. I thought to myself, but the thing is I love someone else now, someone I can really be with. That is so much better than hiding behind closed doors.

Even though he still had a piece of my heart, I was smart enough to know I couldn't live one life in his office and another out in the open like he had managed to do all those years, even if I wanted to. It was time for me to move on. I would still keep this secret, for him and for myself.

I felt I was a bad person and that I fit into the same category as him. I never wanted to face up to that. At the same time I also felt that even though we were over, I would still have a special place in my heart for him and would always be glad for the time I did have with him, because he was after all my "first love."

Chapter Eight

"Moving On"

I now had a little money. Well, a lot of money especially for a teenager. I gave my parents a little for some things they needed. I needed braces. So I paid for my braces, to have four teeth pulled and four teeth cut out. I had way too many teeth. And this was something I had wanted fixed for a long time.

I also decided to buy a new car. The Preacher knew I was looking for one. He called me in his office and said his wife had someone run into the side of her car so they were just going to sell it and get the insurance money. He said, "Your daddy could probably fix it for almost nothing."

He said, "I will sell it to you at a good price." I loved the car so I said, "Let me talk to my dad." My dad told me that he could fix it if I wanted it. So, I paid the Preacher four thousand dollars for this Acura and I spent five hundred dollars on materials for Daddy to fix it. The Preacher collected who knows how much in insurance money.

Daddy had it fixed in a few days, and I was excited. I was driving it to my grandma's and while I was stopped at a train crossing the car cut off. I finally got it started and got home. The next day it did it again so I took it to a mechanic to have it checked. They told me they didn't know what was wrong and that I would need to take it to the Acura dealership, which was an hour away.

I called the Preacher and let him know that I was very disappointed in the car. I asked had he cashed my check yet. He was very irritated but said, "No I haven't cashed it, do you want me to buy the thing back?" I said, "Yes, please, because I don't have the time and extra money to have it fixed." He came over a few hours later and handed me my check.

At the time I never thought about the five hundred dollars that I had paid for Daddy to fix it, plus Daddy's labor. I bet the Preacher thought about it! So, he collected insurance money, and got the body work done for free. This was how he liked to work. Too bad when I realized this it was too late to even bother bringing it up.

A very nice gentleman from church had a Honda civic for sale. This man and his wife were two of the best people you could ever meet, a very sweet, loving couple. He let me know about this car and asked me if I would like to see it. I drove out to their house to look at it. He gave me the keys and told me to take it for a ride. I loved it! When I got back I told him that I really liked it and thought I would like to buy it and that I would let him know at church.

At school the next day the preacher asked me what I thought of the car and I said, "I want it; it drives so good." He said, "Well that's because you're not used to new cars. He is asking too much for it. Don't buy it. I will tell him you don't want it." So true to form, I replied, "Okay."

The following Sunday this sweet man who was selling the car pulled me to the side and asked, "Amanda, did your daddy tell you not to buy the car or the Preacher?" I told him, "The Preacher told me not to buy it." He said, "Okay that's all I wanted to know."

I gathered from this that the Preacher had lied to this man and told him that my daddy didn't want me to buy it. Years later I found out he was jealous of this man if he sold more cars than him or did better in his personal car dealings. Again, there was always a motive behind everything the Preacher said and did. So many times I was in the middle.

Not much longer after that the nice man and his wife had seen and dealt with enough. They were another set of members to leave. The Preacher's flock of sheep was getting smaller and smaller. I think pieces of the puzzle were falling in place for me, but it was more, Okay this man I was involved with for years isn't perfect, nothing to the extent that I later found out.

I had some really good friends in school that he expelled for really dumb things. According to the rule book you would be expelled for going to a movie, or a dance. My two best friends were some of them. They were sisters. Rumors and gossip had spread that the older sister had a boyfriend. It was said that she wasn't following the rule book to the letter.

The Preacher called her out on this. He didn't want to talk about it, or try to help her, or work it out. He just had these two sisters thrown out of school. That day I lost two great friends who still could be in my life today had it not been for him. Also, another great friend of mine had gone to a public school prom with a girl and was expelled on the spot.

This was only more destruction in my life. Not to mention their lives. When members left or were banished, we were expected to cut all ties. These friends were doing good to get out from under his leadership when they did.

Chapter Nine

"Will You Marry Me?"

Eddie and I were young and in love. We had talked about marriage. We knew that we wanted to be together. He talked to my dad to ask for my hand. One Wednesday night after church service we went to the nicest restaurant in town. Eddie got down on one knee and asked, "Will you marry me?" I smiled and said, "Yes!"

We had almost a year before I graduated and he had a year and a half left of college but, I was wearing his ring! The news was buzzing around school and the Preacher walked over to my desk, picked up my hand and looked at the ring and kind of smiled and shook his head. I didn't care what he was thinking. I was happy!

Eddie and I started making plans for a home and a wedding. He was still going to school and had found a better job. As for me, I was a senior in high school planning a wedding.

At this point for some reason the Preacher wanted to get to know my future husband. He would invite Eddie to go fishing and out to eat. Eddie knew I was very insecure and fearful of him looking at other girls, wanting to be with someone else, and worst case cheating on me. Of course I was! The Godliest man we all knew was doing all of these things. I assumed that Eddie, and all males would be the same way.

This was the first problem Eddie and I had that stemmed from the horrible memory that this preacher inflicted on me. Apparently, Eddie spoke to the Preacher about me feeling this way about men. Later, Eddie informed me that the Preacher told him that I must have felt this way because of my daddy. Here my daddy was such a better man than the Preacher but he was taking the blame for what the Preacher had done. Eddie also told me of some of the strange "words of wisdom" from the Preacher, like, "It is good and flattering if other guys or men look at and want your girl." Eddie and I both knew that was a strange thing for a Preacher to say. And wondered why he had said it.

After the Preacher had some of these talks with Eddie, somehow the two of us wound up in the same place alone and he mentioned to me Eddie's concerns. And I told him that I was afraid of Eddie cheating on me or me not being good enough. I told him if Eddie ever did, I wouldn't be able to handle it. He seemed very concerned for me and made the comment, "I guess that's my fault." I said nothing, I only looked at him, but I knew that it was his fault.

One evening we were sitting in service and the Preacher was preaching his sermon. I had what I felt was a message from God. An overwhelming feeling came over me that I needed to tell my future husband about what I had been through and what had happened to me. At least let him know in case he would no longer want to marry me. I felt that I needed to give him the chance to get out if he chose to.

That night he was taking me home, and he parked the car. I told him I needed to tell him something. He could tell I was nervous. I said, "Someone at church messed with me when I was younger." That's all I said. He looked very sad and shocked by the news. He was quiet for a moment and asked, "Was it our teacher?" Our leader on Wednesday nights was the secretary's husband. (We had a class with him every other Wednesday).

He was very shocked when I said, "No, no, no it was the Preacher. I don't want to talk about it, and you have to promise to never say anything. If you don't want to marry me I understand. I feel like I am damaged goods and you deserve better than me." He hugged me and said, "Of course I want to marry you, and I promise I won't say anything." Still I could tell now, not only was this a weight on my shoulders, it was one on his as well. I, however, felt so much better having told Eddie. Though I knew I would never want him to know it all.

My senior year flew by and we had planned to have a June wedding. I had the dress, and everything was ready. Our house was almost done. I was to graduate in early June and be married, June the 30th 2001. I graduated and the ceremony went well. I was glad to be done with school and had decided to be a wife instead of going on to college.

Eddie did as I asked and acted as though he didn't know anything about the Preacher and me, though he still didn't know the whole story or any of the details. We still went to church as usual and our wedding was drawing near.

The preacher told us that he would like to meet with us for marriage counseling. I was thinking this must be a joke! It was set to be right before the rehearsal. We were about ten minutes late and he was mad about it and said, "Well, now we don't have time! Just forget it!" Just like a child. So the counseling never happened and the Preacher was moody throughout the entire evening.

I had told Eddie a few weeks prior that I didn't want the Preacher to marry us. I told him that we should tell the Preacher that he knew and on the day of the wedding he needed to wake up sick and call someone else to marry us. Eddie said, "We shouldn't open a can of worms and start anything." We planned to get married and then leave the church anyway. Keep in mind Eddie had no idea the extent of all that happened. I went ahead and agreed with him.

The next day was our wedding day. I was happy no matter who was marrying us. I was also very blessed to be marrying into such a sweet family. The wedding was very nice but nothing extravagant. I was more interested in the marriage than the wedding.

I could tell that some of our fellow church members didn't seem too happy, and the Preacher most definitely did not. I knew why. Mama was running around getting things ready and she asked me what the Preacher's problem was. Everyone could tell something was eating him. Even in all the pictures, he had a very mad, sour look on his face. I knew the reason. It was because, to him, Eddie was officially stealing me away. He knew now it was over between us for sure and he didn't like it and it showed.

After the wedding Eddie was standing beside the Preacher and the Preacher asked Eddie, "Are you going to stay and help clean up this mess?" Because the Preacher's "followers" didn't have minds of their own, all the church members developed his attitude about our wedding and marriage.

Eddie and I did not stay to clean up. We left for our honeymoon straight away. I talked to mama a while later and she told me that no one from church stayed to help clean up or put things away. She said it was only the family. She told me that they did the best they could but they didn't even know where anything belonged.

This left my family and Eddie's family wondering what the Preacher's deal was and why everyone was acting this way. I would just say, I guess they think we're too young to get married or something like that. But I knew why and I was angry!

Eddie and I went to Tennessee on our honeymoon and had a wonderful time. We got home on a Wednesday night. We stopped by the church to drop off a letter that I had written. It was to the Preacher to let him know we were leaving the church. In that letter I also let him know that he had better not bad mouth us to the congregation. I never said that I had told Eddie anything about what had happened. Eddie delivered the letter and we left.

I did later hear from a member that he would say behind the pulpit that he didn't know or understand why we left. He bragged about how much he had done for me throughout the years. How he paid my tuition in full and so on. When I got a job and started working, I paid my own tuition. He failed to mention that. It was all him and what he had done. When I heard this I thought, If only the church members knew what he had really done to me!

The Preacher's faithful followers were the ones who shunned us and the ones we never heard from, but while we were there claimed to love us so much. I thought to myself many times, Is this what Christianity is all about? I knew it was not. These very people did not figure out for themselves what was right and what was not. They only listened to their preacher.

Either way, no matter about them, Eddie and I were happy and had set up our home. We moved on a piece of land beside Eddie's grandparents. We had started attending a different Baptist church in the hopes that not all preachers were like our former one. I still knew there was a God and there had to be some men in the world who loved Him and were faithful to Him and to their wives.

The pastor of this new church was a very nice man. He was a young man. He had a very sweet wife and all the members welcomed us there at their church. Even as nice as this church and these people were, I was still missing my old church. Not the Preacher or his sermons, but the people; the few who were still my friends and the true, real Christians. Some of the friends that I had made for the last ten years, I missed very much. For these reasons I just couldn't get comfortable at this new church.

During this transition, I got a visit from the Preacher's wife. She came over with my grandma. She made small talk at first and asked to see our wedding pictures. She then began to cry and said, "We really miss you and wish you would come back! The Preacher says he doesn't know why he acted the way he did and he's sorry. Church is not the same without you." I just hugged her said, "Okay." I really didn't know how to take all this. I did know that she was someone very special to me.

Eddie and I had only been married about a month when Eddie's grandmother suddenly passed away. The Preacher's wife, my grandmother and a few other ladies came out and brought food to Eddie's grandparent's house. They asked was there anyone to preach the funeral. We said no one special because they didn't attend church anywhere. The Preacher's wife said, "I'll talk to the Preacher." Eddie and I just looked at each other and said, "Well, okay."

A while later the Preacher came out to Eddie's grandparent's home. He was talking to Eddie's grandpa and Eddie's mother and father. They decided that they would let the Preacher oversee the funeral. He did. And friends from church attended the service. All this really made me see just how much I missed them all.

A week or so later I asked Eddie about going back. I was still very young and naive. I think with so much of my life changing, trying to grow up, getting married, living in a different place, going to a different church, I think I wanted something familiar in my life.

Eddie said it was okay. For him now hindsight is 20-20. He didn't feel at the time that there was any danger. We never talked about that part of the past and he only thought, "Well she's very pretty and at some point the Preacher made some kind of comment or some kind of suggestive action toward her." He later told me this, and I guess it's always what I wanted him to think.

We went back to our former church and all the members were thrilled to see us. We fit right back in. We sat every service beside my grandmother. It wasn't long before the Preacher called me and asked me to help in the school. This took place three days of the week. I was working with the preschoolers and I enjoyed it. The Preacher never tried anything and never even said anything out of the way. There was an unspoken understanding I suppose. Though, sometimes he would come in our classroom and smile and look at me like he had so many times before. I thought nothing of this at the time.

Chapter Ten

"Unexpected News"

Eddie and I had been married for less than six months and we found out that we were expecting a baby. This was very scary, shocking news. Even more so since it was not planned and we were so very young. We had a plan to wait at least three years before starting a family. We did, however, embrace the idea and tried to get used to the thought of being parents.

I was young and afraid, and my hormones were going crazy. As the weeks passed, this seemed to become worse. All of that was starting to take a toll on our relationship. Eddie didn't know what to do. A part of me just wanted to be a kid again, even more so since I had missed out on being a normal teenager and had been forced to grow up so fast. And life itself was moving at lightening speed.

Eddie was working the night shift at this time and I started spending many nights with my grandmother. He wasn't happy that I wasn't always home in the mornings when he got there. This caused tension and arguments. One day I told him that I needed time and wanted to leave for a while. So I moved back in with my grandma for a few weeks. At that time I didn't know what I would do next and Eddie didn't either.

I suppose the Preacher knew all of this from Grandma. He asked to speak to me. We were standing up in front of his desk. I felt maybe he wanted to try to help. I talked to him and explained that everything was happening so fast and I told him how I was feeling. He listened and said that he did want to be my friend. He seemed very concerned for me. He hugged me and said if there was anything I needed to let him know. As I was leaving he leaned into my face and tried to kiss me. I pulled back and just gave him a look that said, "I don't think so!" I was thinking to myself, don't start, I cannot deal with this now. He smiled at me and said, "Okay, it's too soon." I remember thinking, "Too soon? Yeah, as if that's ever going to happen again!"

I just turned around and walked out. I suppose he was hoping even though I had a baby on the way, that Eddie and I would split up and I would be his again. That's how selfish he was. No matter that I would be a single mother to a child with a broken family. He was only thinking of himself as usual.

I tried to get it together. I knew where I needed to be. That was at home with my husband. That's where I went and we were trying to deal with everything and to get ready for the new baby. As the months went by we were happy about it. Still a little frightened by the entire process, but happy.

On June 30, 2002 (our anniversary) our sweet baby girl was born. This was such a wonderful anniversary present. I was only nineteen at the time and Eddie was almost twenty one. We got married young and became parents young. The Preacher and his wife came to the hospital to see the baby. They congratulated us and told us how beautiful she was.

I was breastfeeding the baby at the time and when she was about a week old we started going back to church. I remember the Preacher making me feel very self-conscious because he kept staring at my breasts. So much so, I just knew others had to notice. That was the first inappropriate thing he had done since he tried to kiss me while I was pregnant. This too I overlooked. He came back to the nursery and wanted to hold the baby. I recall this making me feel very awkward. I can't really explain how I felt. I was glad when he gave her back to me.

Eddie and I learned very quickly that being parents was no easy task. Our baby girl brought so much joy to our lives and watching her learn and grow was so much fun, although at times it was a challenge. She was the glue that held or family together and we were so blessed to have her.

Life at church went on. We still did like we thought we had to by attending Sunday morning, Sunday night and

Wednesday night, never missing anything when the doors were open. More members had left. Some new had come and then left. It seemed that the members and funds were lowering all the time. Since I had the baby, I was no longer helping in the school. Eddie finished college while I was pregnant. And he had gotten a good job.

The Preacher had a friend that was the pastor of another church in town. This man left his church in Virginia to pastor a church in Missouri. The two of them had been talking and this friend knew of a church nearby him that needed a pastor. I suppose at this point the wheels in the Preacher's mind were turning. He had nothing left at this church. No extramarital affair, hardly any members and no money.

Our baby was almost a year and a half now. Time was moving on as it tends to do. The Preacher had in the works plans of leaving his church. One day I was at the school doing something while the baby was at home with Eddie, the Preacher asked to speak to me in his office. I remember this gave me butterflies.

I walked in his office and sat down. It still looked the same and still smelled of cologne. He looked at me really seriously and said, "I need to talk to you about something." I said, "Okay, what?" He explained, "My wife and I are leaving." "Leaving?" I asked. He said, "Yes I feel that God is leading me to help a church in Missouri. We will be leaving in a few months."

I was the only one he had told at that point. I was a little shocked by the news. He then said, "I want to be sure that you and Eddie will stay in church." I said, "We will." Though, I did not understand his reasoning behind that. I wondered, Why does he care if we stay in church or not?

The conversation then became a little deeper. He said, "I'm sorry for what I did to you. I hope that you don't hate me." It seemed very sincere, but to this day I don't know how to take it. I said, "No, I don't hate you." I felt a little sorry for him. He looked so very distressed. I walked over to him and took his hand and said, "I could never hate you." Before I knew what was happening, he quickly pulled me to him and kissed me, I pulled back to walk away and he said, "Please come and see me sometime."

51

I walked out and began to cry. (This is the part of my story that is hard to admit. It makes me sick to my stomach, but I want to be honest and get it all out there.) As I was crying I walked straight to the ladies room. I looked at myself in the mirror and thought to myself, I cannot go through this again; I cannot go through this again! I knew then that that wall I had built was slowly tumbling down.

I was struggling with so much anxiety and so many emotions. I couldn't eat and I couldn't sleep. During the next few weeks I lost ten pounds and my mind was constantly racing. I felt as though I were lost.

The Preacher asked me if I would oversee the church's fall festival. I said I would and started making plans for that. I wonder now if maybe that was only a plan to get me there alone during the process of setting up for the fall activities.

I had to be there early to set up the night of the festival. He was there. It seemed he was always there. He came in the room where I was. He said, "Hi!" He stared at me as if to make me feel uncomfortable and self-conscious as he had done many times throughout the years. I'm sure he could tell it made me nervous. He then asked, "Would you just let me hold you for a few minutes?" I hesitated for a minute, but then I agreed. I let him hold me and then he took my face in his hands and he began to kiss me passionately.

I felt as though I would be sick or faint or maybe both. I knew this was all wrong. Fortunately, it was about time for people to start coming for the festival. He went back to his office and I continued what I was doing, still with this pain in my stomach that wouldn't go away. In my mind I knew what was going on between us was not right, but I felt my heart was telling me something very different.

All the children had a good time at the festival and Eddie had brought the baby. She was dressed up like Minnie Mouse. The evening was coming to an end and Eddie took the baby home to get her ready for bed while I stayed to clean up. Before I knew it all the kids were gone, the Preacher's wife was gone, everyone was gone......except him. I was about finished cleaning up when he walked in the room.

He walked over to me and pulled me to him and kissed me. While we were kissing he began to unzip his pants. He then started pushing my head down. I said, "No, I can't!" In an irritated manner, as he zipped his pants he said, "Okay then, you can leave through the back door and I'll go out the other door in a few minutes so it doesn't look suspicious." I wanted to stay and be with him for a few minutes, but not if that was what he wanted me to do. So I left. All the while thinking, is that act all that I am good for? Is that all he wants from me? Does he even care for me at all? Has he ever loved me?

This frame of mind wasn't enough for me to tell him, "no more". I wish it would have been. In the weeks before he left I did meet with him at church alone a few times. I fell right back into the place where I thought this was natural and we were something good and special. Almost nothing would have to be done, for him to be "finished". He could even have me touch him from the outside of his pants while kissing him. And all I wanted to do was please him.

There was never any kind of real satisfaction on my part. I think he loved leaving me wanting more. Though, for me it was more about being with him and just spending time with him, so much more than something sexual. Thirty minutes here and there with him never felt like enough.

I felt horrible after leaving our meetings. I felt I was an awful person, wife and mother. I was. I hated myself and what I was doing. It was wrong on so many levels. I had one part of me in agony that the Preacher and his wife were moving away. Another part of me was glad that they would be gone and maybe it would finally be over. And he would no longer have such a strong hold over me. At least I thought with miles between us that he wouldn't.

I was sort of offended, when in one of our meetings, the Preacher said, "Can I ask you a personal question?" I replied, "Yes". He said, "How often do you and Eddie have sex?" I was a little stunned by that question and wondered where he was going with this. I said two or three times a week, I guess. He replied, "Okay, I was just wondering why you came back to me and if something was wrong between you and your husband." I said, "Eddie is wonderful. I love him and nothing is really lacking in our marriage, I just love you too, I loved you first!" He smiled and said, "Okay." I suppose he couldn't comprehend that my attachment to him was purely emotional. An attachment that I had had really from the time I was eight years old.

In the months prior to the Preacher and his wife moving away, while we were having our secret meetings, I was having dreams, still having stomachaches and feeling bad about myself. I would sometimes think to myself, at least it is almost over. I would think about Eddie being such a good husband and a good father. I hated the thought of doing what I was doing and what it would do to him if he knew. I still had a part of me that felt it was okay. Like what the Preacher had always told me was true. That he and I were the exception to the rule.......special.......meant to be together in one way or another, no matter the people around us or our circumstances.

I remember wishing that I had never told Eddie about the Preacher when we were dating that way it could never look suspicious between the Preacher and me. I put so much thought into these small details and how to make things "right". Everything was so obscure. I thought about how good Eddie treated me. Foot rubs, back rubs, anything I wanted. He was never selfish. I thought how the other man in my life was always selfish. I would think to myself, would he ever rub my feet? Would he ever put me first? The answer was, No, probably not.

The Preacher had told me if he had known he had a chance of being in my life this way again that he would never have made the decision to leave the church. I'm sure that was not because of me or that he loved me. It was because of what he wanted to get from me. At that time I thought, Oh, he does love me! He's happy I came back to him and wishes that he didn't have to go away. It made me want him and want to find a way to be with him even more. I then started to think we could live this hidden life like we had done so many years before. I could still have my marriage to a man I loved dearly, but also have the man that I loved first and who I thought loved me. It still felt too special to be wrong and too special for me to give up.

Before the Preacher left during one of our meetings he looked at me and asked, "If something were to happen with me and my wife and with you and Eddie, would you come away with me? I had no idea what that meant, exactly, but I knew I was married now. I had a daughter and a responsibility. I wasn't fourteen anymore and I could no longer play his fantasy games. I replied, "I can't, I have my daughter." He sighed and said, "I know, you're right. I wish things were different, I wish you were my wife." All this talk made things even harder.

He then said, "I just want you to be happy." But for me, it was one thing for this to be happening in secret, but it would have been totally different for it to be a reality, out in the real world. And I would never want to hurt the people in our lives. I knew all of this, and it was always in the back of my mind.

The time had just about come for the Preacher and his wife to leave us. There was sadness and relief at the same time on my part. Of course all of his followers were lost and heartbroken. I had gone over to the Preacher's house to help his wife pack in the days before the moving truck arrived. The Preacher came home and his wife had her back turned and he looked at me with that look he was so famous for and mouthed, "I love you." He was determined to drag it out until the end.

The final days of him being the pastor of our church had come. Church members helped load their moving truck. He was leaving to pastor a church in the Midwest. He had been there to visit that church, and to preach to the members. Those church members, who needed a pastor, fell in love with the Preacher and his wife.

They purchased a house for the Preacher and his wife and a couple from the church flew all the way down to our town and drove their moving truck to the new town while the Preacher and his wife followed behind in their vehicle. When the Preacher preached his last sermon at our church he bragged about how wonderful he was because he was stepping out by faith, and journeying into the great blue yonder to do "God's will."

I do know it was God's will for him to get away from us. I'm sorry for the members in the new church that got stuck with him for two years. I truly hope that no damage was done while he was there. The secretary's husband then took over preaching at our church until we could get a permanent pastor. We had a few pastor candidates come in to apply for the position. It took a while to get the right one.

About six months after the Preacher and his wife moved away they came back to town for a visit. He called me and asked if he could see me. We arranged to meet, and I saw him twice alone. On these times he did come to my home. Sex wasn't really an option, I guess you'd say. He still had the desire, but he had definitely aged a lot since I was sixteen.

He told me that we should be careful, that he didn't want to jeopardize my life and my family. He said that he didn't want to anger The Lord and acted as though we shouldn't have sex for these reasons. Not that I was asking by any means. Even though now I was a twenty-one year old woman, with him it was just as though I were that thirteen year old girl who had no idea what she was doing. He called the shots and said what would happen when. But his words made me believe that he cared for my security, that he didn't want us to do something so sinful now that I had a family at stake. I thought that was very admirable and it was all because he cared so much.

The first time he came over, I wanted him to hold me and just be with me. I wanted that time we never seemed to have. I still felt safe and comfortable in his arms. He got what he wanted and was afraid to stick around long. The second time, he was more at ease and he told me that he wished we had more time and that I could have come to the door wearing only a robe. He asked me if I remembered the day he laid me on his office floor. He said, "God you were the most beautiful thing I'd ever seen and you still are!" He hadn't lost his touch.

While he and his wife were in town, they came to our house for supper one night, as if we were all just friends or in a normal situation. It was like leading a double life for me. He was accustomed to leading a double life I suppose.

Chapter Eleven

"The Truth Shall Set You Free"

The Preacher and his wife went back home. He would call our home every once in a while to see how we were. If Eddie answered he would talk to him like it was nothing. When talking to me when I was alone he would tell me about their church and say that he missed me and he loved me.

The right pastor (I will call him Pastor Bill so there will be no confusion) for our church was a young man who had a young wife. They had been married about three years. This was their first church. The members voted them in unanimously. They were good people that wanted to serve God.

They moved to Virginia from a city in North Carolina. When the Preacher and his wife left I took over her jobs of cleaning the church and running one of the church buses that picked up children. So, every week I cleaned the church and rode the bus to pick up the children for church. We had Pastor Bill and his wife over for supper on occasion. We got to know them better. They were a big improvement for our church. The church started growing and thriving.

After we voted in our new pastor, it wasn't long and the Preacher and his wife were coming back to town for a visit. I was sitting in the back of the church where we normally sat. I believe Eddie was working that Wednesday evening. The Preacher and his wife walked in the church. It was still early, so not too many people were in the sanctuary yet. After the Preacher talked to a few people, he walked back and sat down behind me. He said, "It's good to see you" as he smiled. I said, "It's good to see you too!" He

said, "Call me and let me know when I can meet with you."
I responded with, "Okay."

The next morning I was driving through a shopping
center parking lot and I saw the Preacher walking by. Our
eyes met and I stopped. He leaned into the car and began
talking. He said, "You look good. I don't remember you
fixing yourself up like this when I was here." I thought to
myself, what's different, more makeup maybe? Does he
think I'm out to find someone to replace him?

I thought this because before he moved away, he and
his wife had been to the church that they were to take over
and met the people. While we were talking once, he
mentioned that all the ladies in the church were very
heavy. I felt like he was telling me that, "so I wouldn't have
to worry" about him getting involved with one of them or
something. Maybe he was thinking out loud and was
disappointed that he wasn't attracted to any of them. I
didn't ask. But I still didn't believe there was ever or would
ever be any "other woman" than me.

Before ending our car side chat he asked, "When can I
see you?"

A few days later, we met. It was the same scenario. He
got what he wanted, something I hated doing, but I did it
for him. He did hang around for a few minutes after to
talk. I didn't want him to leave, but he couldn't stay. The
night before they were to head back to the Midwest, I went
by his mother's house to say goodbye to him and his wife.
I hugged her and we began to cry. His mother and some of
the Preacher's friends were sitting down with the Preacher.

After hugging his wife he stood up to shake my hand
and he then said, "Well shoot, I can hug you Manda." This
was different because we were in front of people and he
always said behind the pulpit that he did not hug women.
(He would criticize men and pastors who were openly
affectionate that way. He, of course, preferred to hide his
affections.) So I was shocked that he hugged me in front of
his wife and others, but to everyone it was completely
innocent. I mean everyone knew that I was like a
granddaughter to him, just like he had always planned.
This way he could be very close to me, even openly and it

would never look strange to others. He and his wife went back to the Midwest the next day.

I began to seriously question myself, my life, my feelings, and my relationship with my husband. I was so distraught that the Preacher was gone again. I was having all of these mixed feelings, emotions and thoughts. I always had this problem just below the surface. I felt that I trusted our new pastor and his wife enough to go speak to them about the feelings that I was having about my situation, though I contemplated talking to them for several weeks before I decided to. I kept thinking if Eddie was the right man for me, then why was I still having these feelings for another man.

The Preacher was gone, but he was still calling me. One day I just cried and told him that something was wrong and that I was really having a hard time. He asked what he could do. I told him that I didn't know. I felt like telling him that I just wanted him to come get me and take me away. He calmed me down and reassured me with his love.

About a week later I called him. He could tell that I was still very upset. He asked me was I feeling guilty because things were happening with us. I replied, "I don't know, I think so, maybe so." He then said, "Well, we'll stop. Maybe that will be better for you. Just don't ever forget that I love you." I agreed to what he said. I was sad, yet relieved at the same time.

I knew that I needed help and that the Preacher could not give it to me. I needed some advice, someone I could talk to. Still not a big talker and very shy, I wrote down some of my feelings and doubts about my marriage. I gave the note to Pastor Bill and his wife. They read it and called me into the office. They always did counseling together, never him alone. This was very smart on his part. I went in there with no intention at all of telling them about my relationship with the Preacher, even though that was the big issue and my big problem.

Pastor Bill said, "No matter what you're feeling, you did not marry the wrong man. God put the two of you together and you have a beautiful family." This was the tough love approach I suppose. He didn't want any of my boohooing. I said, "Okay, you're right", even though that didn't help me. He said, "I'm going to leave now and let you pray with and talk to my wife." He left and I looked at his wife. She smiled and was very sweet.

I had this feeling come over me that was telling me that I NEEDED to tell someone or it would never be over and it would eventually continue to hurt me physically and emotionally. And I would never be free of this man who seemed to have this magical power over me. I looked at her and said, "Our former preacher is not who everyone thinks he is." She immediately got a stone cold look on her face and asked, "What did he do to you?" Her look and question gave me chills.

I told her about how it all started and how we had been in a relationship since I was twelve. I told her how I was confused because I thought my feelings for my husband were different from my feelings for the Preacher. She simply told me, "That's because lust is stronger than love." Also that I was probably so used to the excitement that came from sneaking around with the Preacher that when real love was right in front of me it was harder to see. I knew she was right. She's a very young, but very wise lady. I felt better after telling her and I also was nervous and wondered what would happen next.

She went home and told Pastor Bill. They called me later on in the day and asked me to meet them the next day. I did, and of course they were both still in shock. They had met the preacher when he and his wife had visited a few months prior. And they knew how much all of the church loved and adored him.

Pastor Bill and the Preacher chatted together and Pastor Bill said that the Preacher gave him the scoop on all the members, who to trust, and who to watch out for. Pastor Bill found that so ironic seeing as the Preacher was the one we needed to watch out for.

Pastor Bill told me he never thought in a million years that he would have to deal with something like this. I often felt guilty for putting this burden on him and his wife. He didn't know what to do, especially since I wanted to keep it quiet. I was still looking out for the Preacher and for myself. I just kept thinking about his wife, his mom, my parents, everyone.

I was also thinking how embarrassing it would be if it all had to come out. Pastor Bill asked, "What if he does it or has done it to someone else?" I said, "I truly don't believe that is the case." I really didn't. Pastor Bill tried to put it into perspective for me by comparing my relationship with the Preacher, to a scenario of me and a thirteen year old boy at church. I said that it was not the same. He tried to convince me that it was no different. I still was not convinced because I was blinded by my feelings for the Preacher and the fact that I thought he was a good man and our situation was "special."

One of my arguments in the Preacher's defense was that it would have been different if I were a little girl. I said, "I was under age, but I was almost grown. And the Preacher didn't plan it that way. He didn't seek me out like I was prey." I still could not see how sick it really was. Pastor Bill tried his best to convince me.

He also told me that he wanted to do something. He wanted to shout it from the roof tops, but because I wanted to keep it quiet that he wouldn't do anything at all. He said he would only keep his eyes and ears open in the hopes that if there was anyone else that they too would come forward.

Pastor Bill did have many questions for me. I answered them all honestly except for one and that was the question "Did anything ever happen after you met Eddie or after you two were married." I told him and his wife "No". I felt if they knew something had happened that I would be considered an adulterer. I did feel bad for lying and I knew I could not get all the help that I needed unless I was completely honest. I thought about that the whole night after I got home.

When I went to talk to them the very next day I did confess to them the whole truth. Pastor Bill stated, "Had this happened in bible times, I would have been stoned." I would have been considered an adulterer. I'm sure he was trying to make me realize the severity of the situation at hand and keep me from falling into past sins. He could see that I still harbored feelings for the Preacher. He bluntly asked me, "Do you want the Preacher or do you want your husband?" Deep down I felt that what I really wanted was them both. As I was sobbing, I said, "I want my husband!"

I was crying, and I asked if they hated me, was I horrible? Pastor Bill said, "No, we don't hate you." His wife, who was sitting beside me, began to cry with me and she got down on her knees beside my chair and said, "Amanda, had I been in your situation, I can't say I would have done anything differently." I hugged her and we cried together. To this day that still touches my heart. I will forever be grateful for that Godly lady putting herself in my shoes for those moments.

She and Pastor Bill began prayer sessions and counseling to try to help me. Pastor Bill asked me if he could call the Preacher and try to give him the chance to confess and make that opportunity available for the future. Just talk to him and drop hints that he knew something about him from one of the members. Also to tell him that he would pray for him and that if he needed to talk, he could call anytime. We figured the Preacher would immediately call me to snoop around and see if I had talked. He didn't call me. We found out he did call the secretary and asked her if she knew what our new Pastor's deal was and why he seemed to be accusing him of something.

So then we waited. Pastor Bill told me that he was just about positive that there had been others. I was still in doubt about that. I told Pastor Bill over and over that I didn't believe that. My mind was still clouded with the belief that the Preacher loved me and he didn't intend for things to happen the way they did.

Before the Preacher and his wife left our church, the church gave them a huge going away party. His daughter flew in from California. There was food and singing, people wrote sappy poems and so on. They also had a huge picture of the Pastor framed with a small plaque at the bottom that had his name on it as the founder of the church. They hung that picture in the room that you walked into directly in the side entrance of the church. This was where it would be seen by all. Most people used the side door and not the front.

One of the decisions Pastor Bill made was to have that picture moved to kind of an inconspicuous place. He told me that picture was most definitely not the first thing that I needed to see when I walked in the house of God. He was right and I was happy he moved it. We knew it would cause a bit of a stir with the members. Pastor Bill was taking a stand in the only way he could with me unwilling to go public with my story.

Six or eight months passed by and we found out that the Preacher and his wife were coming to town for a visit. We knew that they would come to church. Pastor Bill had a plan to preach a message about a pastor who had been found out and accused of molesting children. The night came and he preached his sermon loud. It was a way to drop another hint that the Preacher had been found out.

After the closing prayer, the Preacher stood directly up and looked right dead at me, not really like he knew I told, but that he knew I was probably thinking of him throughout the whole sermon. He and his wife left right away.

They went back to their new town and he hadn't tried to contact me while they were in town. I told Pastor Bill and his wife about the look that I got as soon as the service was over. The Preacher talked to members and wondered why Pastor Bill wouldn't ask him to speak or pray while he was visiting. He also noticed that the picture had been moved. He didn't like that at all and you could tell many of the members didn't like it either.

In fact Pastor Bill was taking a lot of heat for not really acknowledging the Preacher in any way while he was there. I suppose that's part of doing the right thing. People had hard feelings toward Pastor Bill for something that they had no idea about. Some thought that he was jealous of the former Preacher. Only three of us knew the truth. And I am sure that the Preacher had to wonder.

One day they would get to know the reason. At that point in time, Pastor Bill was honoring my request to keep my secret unless we had another witness. Pastor Bill said according to the bible he couldn't call the Preacher out because I was the only one who had come forward. So, we watched and waited. When the Preacher and his wife did visit, Pastor Bill was sure not to let him out of his sight. He let me know that while he couldn't really do anything, he could do his best to protect his church by watching every move the Preacher made.

Chapter Twelve

"New Beginnings"

My husband and I had put our house up for sale because after much contemplation, we had made the decision that Eddie would join the Air Force. We had been considering this decision for several years. The Preacher and his wife knew we had been thinking about this. After they moved away, the Preacher had talked to members and people like the secretary asking had Eddie joined and gone away yet. I later found this out and knew why he was asking. He wanted Eddie gone in the hopes that I would be lonely and available to him.

In the meantime we found out that baby number two was one the way. This time it was planned! Our daughter was almost four. We thought it was the right time.

We sold our house about three months before our son was born. We rented a house not too far from where we were already living. We got settled in our new home and we were waiting for the right time for Eddie to enlist in the Air Force.

At this time my dear sweet grandmother was in a nursing home. Her health had been failing her for years. She was suffering from Alzheimer's disease and several other health issues. We were going to see her everyday and other than her health, life was going good for our family.

Unfortunately, things were about to be turned upside down again. Pastor Bill informed me that he had heard that the Preacher and his wife were moving back to town. He also heard that they were going to take another church in a town close by.

I was about eight months pregnant at this time. The Preacher and his wife did in fact move back to town. They found out where we lived and paid us a visit one Saturday evening. This was extremely awkward for me. They visited for only a few minutes and then left.

In October of 2006 our bouncing baby boy was born. We were thrilled and our family was now complete. But around us everything was about to fall apart.

The problem was now right in front of us. The Preacher was living in town and already trying to steal members to join his new church. We had a feeling that the secretary and her family were going to be some of the first to go. The secretary was already showing the school principal how to handle things, "in case she couldn't be there to do them."

Pastor Bill mentioned all this to me. I flat out said, "Well I can stop them from leaving. I'll just tell her what the Preacher had done." Pastor Bill said, "Well I hadn't thought of that." So we made a plan. We had to stop the Preacher from taking another church in case he was in fact one to repeat his wrongdoings. Two years had gone by since I had told Pastor Bill and his wife. Now the time had come and I was ready to do something.

We decided that I would tell the secretary and then call the Preacher and tell him that Pastor Bill and my husband knew. The next day I walked in the secretary's office and told her that I needed to talk to her about something. I said, "I don't know where to begin." I told her that I had the feeling that they were going to transfer to the Preacher's new church. I said, "Before you do, there's something that you should know." She looked at me with concern. I continued, "The Preacher molested me from the time I was twelve years old." There was silence for a few minutes and then she began to cry.

She then recalled the day that she walked in on us. She said, "I remember that day I walked into the church and the Preacher was standing with you. You had the funniest look on your face and for a split second I thought, something is strange here. As soon as I thought it, I thought to myself no, never! He would never do that! I'm so sorry that I didn't act on my first instinct and say something to you."

I told her I didn't think anyone thought he would ever do that. But I do think a lot of people have probably had a time over the years that a thought passed through their minds as well. Unfortunately, no one acted on it or did anything to find out for sure. Had they done or said something maybe things would not have gotten so out of control for me.

I let the secretary know that Pastor Bill had known for the past two years. I told her we needed to stop the Preacher from taking yet another church. She agreed. I told her that Pastor Bill said he was available if she needed to talk.

She was very upset. She had been attending this man's church for almost twenty years. She was also a best friend to his wife and a good friend to his daughter. She began asking me questions and was very concerned for me. We talked about it until we were exhausted and tried to figure out what needed to be done next.

The secretary then told me about how he would tell people that I had such a hard childhood and that I must have been abused. After me coming out of his office he would say how he felt sorry for me. That he wanted to help me. That was his way of protecting himself....making me seem to be the troubled one. It was all starting to make sense to me. She also said that after Eddie and I started dating that he would drive by my grandmother's house to see if we were there alone. The secretary thought this was strange. At the same time she thought he was trying to look out for me.

Chapter Thirteen

"The Truth Is Out"

I went home, did like we had planned, and called the Preacher. I simply told him, "Pastor Bill and my husband know what happened between us." He asked, "What do you mean?" I slowly said again, "Pastor Bill and my husband know what happened between us." I hung up. My heart was pounding and I was scared to death of what would happen next. A minute later his wife called me back. She sounded very strange when she said, "The Preacher didn't know what you meant." I said, "Let me speak to him please!" He said, "Hello." I asked him, "Why did you have her call me? I told you, my pastor knows and my husband knows!"

He then said, "You mean they know about the day that you asked me out to your house and you sat down beside me and ran your hand up and down my leg? Why are you doing this to me now when I'm getting ready to take a church?" I asked, "Do you really think a man like you needs to take another church?" I felt his wife was right there with him during this conversation.

I hung up. I knew what he was doing. He was trying to make it seem as though I seduced him and that I was the one who went after him as an adult. A minute later, the phone rang again and this time Eddie answered. The Preacher's wife was on the other end, and Eddie simply said, "Neither one of you call back here again." My original plan was to keep the Preacher out of yet another church. That's why I told the secretary and that's why I told the Preacher that I had spoken out. That was as far as I really wanted it to go. The Preacher decided to play ugly and that's when things got out of my control. I only meant for the Preacher to realize what was going on. But he immediately got his wife involved to hide behind her belief in him.

Later that afternoon Eddie and I went to meet with Pastor Bill to talk this through. As I cried, I confessed to Eddie the things that had happened after we were married and that it had been years ago. I tried to make him understand that if this man had not played with my heart, my mind and my body when I was a young girl that he could have come after me full force when I was a twenty year old woman and it would have never happened.

Still at this time the plan was to keep the Preacher from taking another church. We knew if he had another leadership position, there was a chance of him taking advantage of someone else. I still didn't think he was capable of that, but I knew that we were doing the right thing just to be on the safe side.

Eddie wanted to know every detail of the past from start to finish, everything that the Preacher had done to me. This was a long, excruciating, difficult process but we got through it. Eddie stood with me through all the tears and heartache. It was very hard on him and we now had much to work through for months to come.

To say the least this was a rough patch in our marriage. Eddie did go a little crazy. Even to the point of staking out the Preacher's house and threatening him, without the words. I thought for a while that Eddie was going to kill the Preacher and then leave me. The word divorce had come up. I understood that he needed time to process it all. He wondered what was wrong in our marriage that I turned to my abuser. He didn't believe me at first when I said there was no intercourse after he and I were married. Eddie thought that it must have been sexual. He thought that I must have gotten something from the Preacher.

What Eddie didn't know and understand at this time was that my relationship with the Preacher was one sided, all give and no take for me. Eddie didn't see and understand the emotional abuse. I didn't even see and really understand it at that point.

I begged, pleaded, and cried for Eddie to forgive me, for him to try to see it all from my point of view. I tried to make him see the Preacher had this emotional hold over me, a hold that even I didn't fully understand. I suffered from a lot of confusion from the time I was barely thirteen years old. And these attachments that I had to him were more emotional than sexual.

Even though Eddie said he forgave me, he still wanted to take our children to have a paternity test done. That broke my heart. That was a horrible day for me, but I understood. If I were in his shoes I would have done the same. I think as the years have passed he understands more and more the damage that emotional abuse can cause. And of course those precious children are his. I know it gave him peace of mind to have proof.

We found out in the next few days after I broke my silence and let the Preacher know that I had, that the Preacher was calling everyone that he thought would be on his side. He was rallying his troops. He went to his mom and told her that I was spreading lies about him. His daughter flew in to support her daddy. He called his wife's family and anyone he thought he could get to first. He told them that I was always a troubled girl and now I had really lost it. I thought to myself, that idiot, it never had to go farther than Pastor Bill, my husband, the secretary and himself.

The Preacher had his wife call Pastor Bill to try to find out why I was "telling these lies." Also to try to convince him that I had put the moves on him and I was mad because he didn't want me. The secretary who was close to me was there at the time. I told her all this after Pastor Bill let me know what was said. Now it was a battle.......my word against his.

Now that Eddie knew everything, he told me, "I either want him dead or in jail." Pastor Bill called me and said that the Preacher's wife had called him and asked if the Preacher were to sign something that stated he would leave town and never pastor a church again would we not press charges. We said, "Absolutely not." I had to honor my husband's wishes and do my best to get this criminal behind bars. The Preacher knew what he was doing in hiding behind his wife. She was already fighting for him, though she claimed that she didn't believe my "lies". I knew deep in my heart that what Eddie wanted was going to be a horrendous process but I had to do it.

The next day was Sunday. At this time it had been announced to the church what was going on. A much older friend of mine wanted to meet with me. She said she needed to talk to me about something. We sat down and she said, "I can't let you go through this alone. I was a victim too."

She said, "The Preacher did the same thing to me. I tried to fight him for a long time, but he would not take no for an answer. He had me convinced that he loved me. I finally gave in to his charm."

Though she was a grown woman when it started, it was still manipulation. She would get advice or talk about a problem; he would become her friend. Gradually over time he would say bad things about her husband and how he wasn't good enough to her. Then it led to "I can't help myself, I've fallen in love with you."

She told me she had never had a man look at her or to kiss her the way that he did. I knew that he was very good.....he knew what he was doing and he had done it many times. A part of me was extremely shocked at what I was hearing from her. Another part of me already knew and was not at all surprised. She was in fact one of the ones I thought may have been involved with him had there been someone else. It was now confirmed.

I was hurt and angry to say the least. I felt as though someone had just told me that I had been cheated on as if I were the Preacher's wife. More and more I was seeing how horrible he was. More and more I was seeing that I was only someone that he used, not loved. More and more I was seeing how all those years of my life were wasted and not at all years that I should hold dear as I had always done.

My friend claimed it went on for a short while and then she ended it. She was a lot like me. She thought she had been the only one. He had her convinced that she was the only one and he didn't mean for it to happen. Just like me. When she ended things with him, the Preacher apologized and said he wouldn't bother her again. She forgave him and they moved on. She said that if I pressed charges she

71

would stand with me. She had a lot to lose by speaking out, but she did it just the same.

This bonded us in a sense, and we now had proof that the Preacher was the scum of the earth. To top it all, the time frame with my friend and I was the same; though with me it lasted much longer, it began for us both around the same time. To me what is strange is that she attended the church for ten years before he ever tried anything with her. I suppose to him, timing was everything. He had to wait for the perfect time to make his move.

Knowing all this about my friend, the time frame, and all that happened raised so many questions in my mind. I found myself for years trying to analyze that time in my life. Trying to figure out why the Preacher was this way, if he had always been a womanizer and a pervert, and if not, what made him that way? Were women and power the whole reason he started a church? Was he even a born again child of God? Did he even believe in God? Was I the last one when I was a grown woman, or was there someone in the Midwest after me? How did he have me convinced that he loved me all those years, was I that gullible and naive? So many questions and no answers, no closure, nothing.

I later spoke to another woman whom I suspected something could have happened with. She admitted to me that he tried things with her when she and her husband were going through a divorce. She also said that she had suspicions about the Preacher and me because she realized how he was. He had played the same game with her, except for them it was more about the physical part. She said it didn't get so far as for him to say he loved her. And she said there was only oral sex and that even though he wanted her to, she never met him at a hotel.

This lady said that she felt guilty and wanted to confess and let his wife know. The Preacher told her with all the men everyone knew she had been with that no one would believe her over him. She stayed quiet because she knew it was a losing battle. She too had made mistakes in her life, so she realized he was only human and humans make mistakes.

I came to the conclusion that he knew he was safe with me because he had covered his tracks and told everyone that I was troubled and disturbed. Even if I told, he assumed no one would believe me. He thought he was safe with my friend who came forward because she believed they were in love and she had so much to lose if she ever told. She had a wonderful husband and children at home so she would never give herself away, or so he thought. She is a much braver person than he gave her credit for.

He was safe with the lady who was going through the divorce because, according to him, her credibility was no good. He had no idea that someone would speak out and there would be a domino effect. He was a very brave, very stupid man.

I admire these two women so much. They could have kept quiet to save themselves and their own reputations, since they were married Christian women. But they chose to do the right thing and not have me stand alone to face all of the Preacher's ridiculous accusations about my sanity and what kind of person I was.

Even if I had been the only one, or the only one who had come forward, anyone who knew me also knew what he was saying was absurd. If I were the only one, the truth was still the truth. I knew, he knew and more importantly God knew what that truth was.

The secretary, who was like a second mom to me, stood behind me and believed what I was saying. The preacher's wife was supposed to go shopping with the secretary one day around this time (at this point the preacher's wife and his family didn't know that others had come forward and they were holding onto the hope that I was lying). The secretary's husband called the preacher's wife and told her that his wife couldn't see her now. She started crying and asked why they believed it.

The preacher's daughter, who had been very good friends with the secretary as well, left the secretary a hateful voice mail about not being a good friend and Christian by not supporting her daddy. Little did he or his daughter know that it was not only "the crazy little girl" speaking out, but two other women as well. They still thought and hoped that maybe all this was a lie. Deep down they had to have their doubts about that.

The Preacher's wife and his sister went to meet with Pastor Bill, to hear firsthand what all was being said. Pastor Bill later told me about this meeting. He said that when the two ladies came to his home, he could tell that they were both furious and convinced that I was lying. They demanded answers. Pastor Bill said it was terribly hard for him to tell the Preacher's wife that her godly husband had cheated on her for many years.

He compared it to having to tell a wife whose husband had been off at war that her husband had been killed. He told the Preacher's wife that I wasn't the only one who had come forward. When he said that, their anger turned to despair. They knew then that I must have been telling the truth. The Preacher's wife said my friend's name and asked, "Was it her?" Pastor Bill didn't have to answer; she already knew. She began to cry. She asked, "What could I have done to please him more?" Pastor Bill said that's when he only wanted to try to comfort her. He said he hated having to tell her something that her husband should have told her.

When I heard all this from Pastor Bill it made me so sad for the Preacher's wife. She was such a good lady, and she deserved a much better man than the one she married. Her saying these things proved that she believed it. With three women saying the same thing, she couldn't help but believe it. Although, I couldn't help but think then and now, what if I were the only one? What if I were the only one he hurt or the only one who spoke out? I had so many people, even the secretary's husband, mention that because I wasn't the only one, they believed it. This really offended me because even if I were the only one, I would have absolutely no reason to make such a story up. Even the Preacher's wife knew me well enough to know that. She simply did not want to believe it.

Eddie took me to the police station to give my statement. I hated telling a stranger face to face all these intimate details of my situation. It was so much more than just embarrassing. The case was open and the detective was to go question the Preacher the following Monday.

That meant over the weekend I had to tell my parents. Something I had been dreading for weeks. I didn't know how I would tell my parents something so awful.

Eddie was still very upset. He had informed me that he had called the Preacher to ask him exactly what happened when he came to our home. He lied to Eddie and told him that he only came out to see the baby and then left. He tried to make Eddie feel sorry for him by telling him that his wife may leave him. He asked why we were doing this to him. Needless to say, Eddie had no sympathy for him.

We also heard through some of the Preacher's family that while his wife had left him (for only a few short days), he had attempted suicide, but the bullet was a blank. I found this to be laughable. I knew that he was too much of a coward to commit suicide. He was only trying to get his wife's and his family's sympathy.

My parents had moved into my grandmother's house and my sister and I had gone over to help get some work done. I had told my sister prior to this day. I told her that I wanted her with me when I told Mama and Daddy. The whole day had gone by and I kept putting it off. Finally, I had to get home to Eddie and the kids, so I couldn't put it off any longer.

I wanted to tell Mama alone first. I said, "Mama come sit down for a minute." She then replied, "What's wrong?" I guess she could tell. After I mustered up the nerve, I said, "The Preacher molested me when I was younger." She screamed, "What?" She began to sob and asked, "Why didn't you tell me, why didn't you tell me?" I said, "I didn't want to. I thought I was in love with him." She said, "Oh my God, oh my God!! Your daddy is going to have a conniption! Your daddy has always hated that man!"

My heart was pounding. I knew that I had to tell daddy next. Mama went to get him from outside. She looked at me and said, "Tell him" I shook my head and said, "I can't, you tell him." Mama looked at him and said, "That Preacher molested her!"

Daddy turned red and I could see his heart beating through his shirt. He looked at my sister and asked, "You too?" She said, "No." I then said, "If it had been her, I would kill him myself."

Daddy started to pace back and forth. There was silence for a minute and then he stated, "If you had told me this, ten years ago I would have had NO problem marching in that church house and blowing his head off!" He paused and said, "But I am older and wiser now and I will not go to jail for his sorry behind."

I said, "Daddy, it's okay. You don't have to kill him; they're going to arrest him soon." That's the only silver lining that any of us had, the only thing keeping my family and Eddie from going crazy.

Mama later told me of the fights that she and Daddy were having. He was blaming her because he had told her for years that I was too involved in church and they should make me stay at home and spend time with the family more. She would argue and say I loved the church and it was a good place for me to spend my time.

After they both knew, Daddy told Mama, "I told you Amanda spent too much time in that church!" Mama replied, "Keep in mind if you had been the daddy you should have been, she wouldn't have been in his office in the first place!"

Hearing this broke my heart. I told Mama that it wasn't their fault! It is no one's fault but the Preacher's. At one time or another we all felt the blame. I thought about the day he said, "When I hug you it makes me want to do other things," I should have said, yes I will tell, or just told. It would have spared my family and me a lot of heartache in the years to come.

A few days later my parents and I were talking. Daddy said to me, "I have always hated that man! I'll never forget one day he came and invited me to church when you were little. We talked for a while. Later your grandma told me that the Preacher told her that I said that I would never quit drinking for God or for anybody. I never said anything of the sorts. That man flat out lied about me!" I wondered why Daddy had never told me this before. I suppose that is one reason he never liked the Preacher. The Preacher definitely had a way of acting so much better than others because of his so called Christianity.

I recall this attitude rubbing off on me as a young teenager. I remember many times thinking badly of my parents and the company that my Daddy sometimes kept. And I became a little stuck up and developed a "holier-than-thou" attitude. That all stemmed directly from the Preacher, the church and their teachings. That's something else that I regret. I thought that if you didn't attend church and "serve God" that you were no good. I'm sorry to the ones around me at that time in my life that I may have treated badly. I'm sorry for the wedge that it put between loved ones and me. I have learned how very wrong that way of thinking was. I have come to believe that often times Christians with this attitude are the ones who you need to watch out for.

The detective contacted me and said that we could try to get some information by calling the Preacher and taping the conversation. The detective sprung this on me. He didn't tell me what I should say to the Preacher or how I should go about this conversation. I remember just being friendly so as to not be suspicious. I asked him why he told his mother. He said, "I wanted to tell her before someone else did." (He told his mother that Amanda was spreading lies) I then asked him, "Why did you do that to me for all those years?" He said, "Now Manda, it wasn't like that." I thought to myself, Oh really? Then how was it? I wanted to ask him about the other women. I still wish today that I had, just to see what he would have to say for himself and what kind of lies or excuses that he would tell me.

I then said, "Well, maybe if you would least ask for my forgiveness then I could move forward." He replied, "Will you forgive me?" This tactic didn't work. It was a failure. The equipment wasn't working well and you couldn't really hear what was said. I believe that we needed a better detective on the case.

The detective called me the next day and said that he needed me to come down and speak to an attorney. This meeting was going to be set up the way it would be in a courtroom with the prosecutor and defense attorney asking me questions.

I told the whole story to a group of eight or ten strangers. I had what would have been my attorney acting as the Preacher's defense asking me questions in a harassing manner, as I was sobbing and trying to speak at the same time. The attorney looked at me and said, "Understand this is what it will be like!" I told him, "I understand." And really began to realize how difficult the trial was going to be. When we left the attorney, who had ironically visited our church before, (he told me I looked familiar. I realized halfway through the meeting why I looked familiar to him, was because he had been to our church a few months prior to this) I spoke to the detective. He said he had gone to the Preacher's house to try to get him to come in for questioning. He refused, of course. The Preacher told the detective that he could speak to his lawyer.

The detective found out that the Preacher had already put his house, his cars, and any assets in his wife's name. He had also put his house up for sale. These were not the actions of an innocent man. He was proving his guilt! And I suppose the Preacher thought I was like him. I was not after anything of his. I would never take him to civil court and take anything from him and I definitely wouldn't want to pull the rug out from under his wife that way. The issue to Eddie and my family was not money, but right and wrong. He broke the law by doing what he did to me. He hurt me and he hurt my family. His little bit of money wouldn't change, that and it would not make it better.

A week or so later the Preacher had some sort of nervous breakdown and was put in the hospital. His daughter called Pastor Bill and said that she had a confession for me and one of the other ladies. She wanted to meet at church. We all met over at the church one evening with the Preacher's daughter and his sister.

First the Preacher's daughter and his sister talked with Pastor Bill, the other lady (my friend) who had been involved with the Preacher and this lady's husband. The Preacher's confession was that he had started something with this lady. They met at a hotel. She went to the bathroom to change and came back out. He then said he couldn't do it and left her there. He even said that this lady had his wife babysit her child for their little meeting. He was still trying to make out like he had ultimately done nothing wrong.

The Preacher's daughter then told my friend, "If you had come forward then my Dad could have maybe gotten the help that he needed." My friend has said to me on many occasions that she wished she had gone straight to her husband. I have thought if she had gone forward and shown the church who the Preacher was, then I would have been spared. I try not to be bitter for all that could have happened to make things different, but didn't.

Next Eddie, Pastor Bill, the Preacher's daughter, his sister, and I sat down for his daughter to tell us what her dad had to say. She read what he had written down. It stated, "I went to Amanda's house to visit with her and see the baby, while we were sitting on the couch she ran her hand up my leg and I told her, no we won't do this and then I left."

I just looked at his daughter and sister and said, "He's lying." I asked if he admitted to an affair with the other woman and they said, "Yes". I simply said, "I see, because she was of age, right?" They then asked me what my side of the story was. I told them and then his sister asked, "Was there intercourse?" I said, "He tried." She then asked, in a hateful manner, "What do you mean he tried?" I replied, "He tried! It was attempted but didn't completely happen!" I felt as though I was being treated like the criminal instead of the victim.

His daughter was almost crying when she made the comment, "My dad never touched me!" His daughter then told me that her dad was in the hospital and that he may die. She said that I didn't need to spread gossip. I believe she was trying to make me feel sympathy for a man who deserved none. My reply to that was, "If what I say can help someone else, it is not gossip." She was trying to protect her daddy's name even though she had proof that he was a sexual predator. Though she did tell me that she was sorry for what happened to me. She told me that she would pray for my healing. This led me to believe that she did indeed believe my story, even though it must have been hard.

We were waiting to hear from the detective again. He had talked to the other two women. He also talked to Eddie, the Pastor, and my parents. My mom told me that

79

the detective told Daddy that he knew they wanted the Preacher in jail and he knew Eddie wanted him in jail but he wasn't convinced that I wanted him in jail.

This angered me. I told my mother, "I don't know what more everyone wants from me!" I had already gone through hell and back by going forward. Whether I wanted him in jail or not didn't matter. I did what everyone wanted me to do and I wasn't going to back down from that. The detective called and told me that the case was about to go in front of the grand jury and he was going to try to get them to allow me to testify. I know he was worried about the case because it wasn't a typical child abuse case, since I was in love with him and the relationship carried on into adulthood. I know many people can't understand that. My testimony wasn't allowed.

We heard that the Preacher was now out of the hospital and it had been confirmed when Mama called me and told me that Daddy had just called her. She said that he could barely speak for the shaking in his voice. Daddy told her that he had run into the Preacher and his wife at a shopping center. Daddy saw the Preacher's wife go into the store. Daddy looked and saw that the Preacher was sitting in his truck and his windows were down.

Daddy walked up to the truck, he said it took every bit of strength and control he could muster up not to drag the Preacher out of that truck and beat the life out of him. He simply looked at him and pointed his finger in his face and said, "You better hope and pray that the justice system comes through for us, because MY way will not be as easy"! The Preacher said not one word. Even though Daddy wanted to hurt him severely, I think he got some satisfaction just from the fear in the Preacher's eyes. He then confronted the Preacher's wife as she walked out of the store to be sure she heard from him exactly what her husband had done to his daughter. She said nothing.

A few days later the detective came by our home after the case had been presented to the grand jury. He said that the case was thrown out of court. I guess that meant that, to the jury, it wasn't believable. They didn't think the case would be won, or that I wouldn't follow through with the case. The detective told me if they would have let me testify and could have seen me and heard me tell my story that it would not have been thrown out.

He also said that if someone else came forward that was a minor at the time of my abuse that the case could be reopened. He said, "You could still take him to civil court." I said I wasn't interested in that. As I said before I was not going to take anymore away from his wife. She had lost enough. As the detective left my home he stated very sincerely, "I want you to know that I believe you, I believe you." I knew that meant that the jury felt that my story was fabricated and that I was just a woman scorned who was lying about some man who did me wrong.

Or maybe they thought that at the time of the abuse I could even have been one of those thirteen year old girls who ran around doing any and everything. The detective never said all this, but him saying over and over, "If they could have just seen you, they could look at you and tell what kind of person you are and see that you are telling the truth", made me realize what the jury must have been thinking. I thought to myself when the detective left, I don't care if you believe me or not and I don't care if the jury believes me or not. I know what the truth is.

My family and I didn't understand how this could be. How the grand jury could just turn this case away and let a child molester go free. We all just chalked it up to the justice system today. We all hated to hear it, but I knew there had to be a reason. I knew in my heart that God simply didn't want me to have to go through with that, because it would have been very awful and very painful. Maybe He knew that I couldn't handle the pressure of going through with what a courtroom battle would have caused.

The Preacher's niece (the school principal) saw his wife a little while after this. His wife told his niece that they had the house up for sale and that she had to pack up everything herself because the Preacher was hiding out. He wouldn't step foot in the house for fear my daddy was going to blow it up. He might have been free from the law but he wasn't free from the fear, the guilt, and the worry. These things were eating him alive.

He led people to believe that he was a Godly man, a "man's man" as he always liked to say. In reality he in no way is or ever was a real man and he loved no one but himself. He didn't love God, he didn't love his wife, he didn't love me, and he didn't love any of the other girls or women that he made believe they were "the only ones." I don't think he was capable of love. He "loved" me into doing things for him. He was always kind and gentle. I know there were some that he threatened into doing what he wanted.

I found out after struggling with the end result of this book that another minor had come forward. I felt impressed to speak to this particular lady. She just happened to be one that I didn't think of four years ago when I was contacting other potential victims.

We talked and she told me her story. She was fourteen when it started. She was four years older than me, so she was before me. She sought help from her Preacher for sexual abuse at home. He told her, "You have to obey your parents and do just what they say or God will punish you." Then it turned into, "Now you have to do what I say, or I will tell your mom and dad that you told on them." When she told me this, I thought, My God! This is a whole new level of crazy! It blew me away honestly. I knew he was a bad man, but I didn't know until that phone conversation just how purely evil he really was. That was a day that I would have loved to get my hands around his neck! And that was the day that my healing truly began. That was the day that I finally saw the Preacher for the monster that he is.

This lady told me she always hated him and what he made her do, but she was trapped. He turned her life upside down, but she never told anyone except her future husband and then me when I asked her all these years later. Her story broke my heart. It hurt me, but it helped me. I now had proof of another minor who he had horribly hurt. Our situations were the same, yet different. I loved him. She hated him. I don't know which was worse, loving him or hating him. After hearing her story, I felt I did have some closure. I now KNEW that he had to be mentally ill. It was one thing to pretend to love a young teenager and manipulate her that way, but it's another thing to threaten and hurt one who had already been hurt and who was coming to you for help.

Chapter Fourteen

"Healing Our Wounds"

Now that we knew the police weren't going to arrest him and no justice was going to be served. We were all wondering what we do now. The answer was, try to heal and try to move on the best we can. That could not happen soon enough.

For Mama and Daddy this was not good enough. It was not acceptable that this man had gotten away with what he had done! Mama said, "There have to be other young girls. We need to try to find them."

I searched for former members and old friends. Anyone that I thought could have been a possible victim. A few of the girls said that he made them uncomfortable. One said she was crying once and he hugged her. That was it. This was as far as we got with the eight to ten girls that I talked to. These were all my age or a little older than me. There was an eight year gap prior to when it started happening to me and when the Preacher started the church. We still wonder how many other victims may be out there.

A few weeks after all this, my mama read in the city paper that the upcoming Sunday was Pastor Appreciation Day. Of course seeing this sent chills up her spine. She wanted to do something to let our city know that there was one pastor that we could not appreciate. My parents went to the police station to see if it would be considered slander if they put an article about our "beloved pastor" next to all of the pastors that the paper would be honoring. They said as long as we worded it carefully it would be okay.

The newspaper refused to print it because they felt for their sake it was too risky. So my parents decided to print their planned article onto flyers and go to every church in town and place them on every car in the parking lots. They got a small bit of satisfaction in doing this. Also, they held the hope that it may bring out other victims.

I suffered a little blame for this from some of the church members who were trying to protect the Preacher's elderly mother who still attended the church and who received a flyer. I was told that the wrong people were being hurt. I said I understood what they meant, but that they needed to understand that my parent's flyers didn't hurt anyone. The Preacher did. The flyers were simply one effect of the cause. I was and am sorry for his mama still today. I am sure she never thought that she would see the day that her son would be found to be a child molester.

The Preacher and his wife left their house (still up for sale) and ran to hide in another state where he had some extended family. They knew they could not stay in town for fear of seeing someone and being confronted. To this day, that's where they still are. From what I hear he has had several strokes and has many health problems. His wife is being true to her vows and standing by his side and taking care of him. I admire her for even being able to stand the sight of him. She is a very good woman. I am sure that she is sorry for what happened. I thought that one day I would get an apology from one of them, but that day has not come.

We were all trying to move on and recover from this coming out. The whole church now knew and some of the members were very supportive of me. With a lot of church members, they believe you forgive and forget, and let it go. My parents, my husband, my sister, my brother and I couldn't do that.

My parents were not forgiving or forgetting. Having a daughter myself, I understood that completely. Some people weren't open minded enough to think, "What if I were in their shoes?" Pastor Bill had known for two years. I of course had known for eleven years, though I had just gotten proof that there were in fact other women and that he wasn't a man who accidentally fell in love with me and made a mistake when he acted on it. My parents had just found out. It was still very raw to them.

What he did was illegal, immoral, and wrong. I still felt that if I had been the only one that there may have been a part of me that could excuse it or forgive him. No one else could I'm sure. I thought I knew him. He was such a huge part of my life for many years. Finding out that I had not only been manipulated, taken advantage of and abused, but flat out lied to as well, was still a raw sore to me and one more thing that I had to work through.

When I first told Pastor Bill and his wife, they counseled with me. I told them that the Preacher was my first love. They told me it wasn't love. He was a man who did bad things. He didn't love me. I still defended him. Even with all their counseling and talking and praying, I defended him and believed what I believed. I believed what he programmed me to believe for all those years.

Now that I know the truth, I finally realize that he was and is a very bad man who stole so much from me. He told me nothing but lies and he got away with it for many years, far more than he should have. If I had been the ONLY one, I could have at least felt that my love wasn't wasted and that maybe he did love me in his own way. With there being others and so many lies, I can't even tell myself that. The legal system let him go and he got away with a crime, but now his whole family knows what he did.

This all came out in March 2007. My grandmother wasn't in her right mind enough to understand what was going on. We were glad that we never had to tell her. She would have been absolutely devastated. I believe even more than that she would have been furious. I am glad that she never saw the day that a man she loved and trusted turned out to be a man who did such horrible things.

I am sorry for all the people in his life that did see that day and have to live with it. He had everyone fooled. His family and loved ones don't even recognize him. I often wonder if he ever admitted to anyone about what he had done to me and with all the others. The truth is still the truth no matter how many lies are told to try to change it or cover it up. I hope he finally realized that. He has yet to ask my forgiveness and that is most likely because he's not sorry. I believe he's only sorry that he was found out. And even more than that, probably angry that I didn't keep his secret and love him until death.

I am sure he hates me with a passion. After I spoke out his world went crashing down. I don't have to feel any guilt for that. He caused that, not me. I hope in speaking out that I stopped him from scarring another girl, daughter, wife, and mother. Once damage like that is done, it's done. I can forgive, but I'll never be able to forget, no matter how hard I try or how badly I would like to.

My grandmother passed away in June 2007. We knew she was ready to go join my papa at her home in heaven. We know she is now in her right mind and is at peace. She suffered for a long time. We were so sad to let her go, but we had a sense of relief as well. I'm not sure how it is when we reach heaven. But I hope she never had to learn the information that is burned into her family's memory.

Chapter Fifteen

"Getting on With Our Lives"

Now that the Preacher was finally out of town again and out of the picture Eddie enlisted in the Air Force. We said goodbye to him as he was going to basic training and would be gone for six months. His first duty station was out west. He was to attend the Defense Language Institute. We were already so proud of him and of the terrific job we knew he was going to do.

The time came for the children and I to say goodbye to our family and hometown. We were off to join Eddie. We were sad, but at the same time very excited. It was such a wonderful experience. Even though it was so far from home we enjoyed our two years there. We felt as though we were seeing the world!

In those two years Eddie learned two languages and it was time to move forward for more training. He needed to be in another state for five months. The military wouldn't move the children and me so we decided it best to go spend time with family while he had to be away.

So our now seven year old daughter, three year old son and I loaded up in our car to follow behind my husband in his truck to drive across the US. We stopped in Los Angeles; saw the Grand Canyon and many of God's masterpieces on our trip. We had to leave Eddie in Texas. The children and I drove the rest of the way to our old hometown. This was one of the best experiences of my life. I would love to make a cross country trip again someday.

We were happy to be home with our family. It was so good to see my parents, my brother and sister, my nephews and in laws. The children were so glad to see everyone as well. It was great to be home.

We all enjoyed so much quality time together that I will be forever grateful for. The best part is the Preacher was in the past and far from our minds. My sister, her husband, and their boys lived in town and my brother lived right up the road from my parents. We were able to see everyone everyday.

Our family was able to go on a wonderful beach vacation and spend a week together at a beach house. My sister, my brother-in-law, my brother, and I would go for walks on the beach at night after the children were in bed at the house with my parents. Amazing memories like these are what I hope will someday completely overshadow all of my bad memories from my past.

Before we knew it, our five months home were over, and it was time to move to Eddie's next duty station in the northern Midwest. We had to say goodbye to everyone all over again. It was okay because we knew we would see everyone in about six months for Christmas. At least we thought we would.

Five months after being in the new town my husband got a phone call while the children and I were in the car with him. Eddie saw that it was my mom's number so he let me answer it. On the other end of the line was my brother in law. He asked to speak to Eddie. I heard Eddie say, "Okay I'll talk to you in a few minutes."

My heart sank into my stomach. I knew something was wrong. I was sick to my stomach the twenty minutes between dropping Eddie off and picking him back up. I knew the news had to do with either my daddy, or my brother who suffered from liver problems.

Eddie got into the car and I asked, "What is going on?" He replied, "I didn't talk to him yet. I tried to call back, but he didn't answer." I then said, "I know you're lying, tell me now!" He paused for a minute and then whispered, "It's Donnie." I remember yelling, "What? What? What is it?"

Eddie began to cry and said, "He killed himself." I just started screaming, "No, no" over and over. My mind was racing with questions, and I screamed and sobbed the whole way home while Eddie tried to calm the kids. I thought it was a drug overdose, I knew that had to be it. I knew it must have been an accident. My wonderful, smart, loving brother would never do this to us. Not on purpose. Whether drugs or alcohol were a factor, I found out that that great man put a pistol in his mouth. That by far was the worst day of my life, followed by the worst months.

The kids and I flew home the next day. I began helping my family plan for a service for my sweet brother. None of us could believe this was happening. It felt as though we were all wandering around in a cloudy haze. It was a nightmare.

I still go through the hell of thinking that I let my brother down somehow. Not a day goes by that I don't think about it and wonder why it had to be this way.

My brother was so loving and very protective of my sister and me. He hated what the Preacher had done to me. His girlfriend told me that if the subject ever came up, he would become so angry. I remember that he always thought there was something disturbing about the Preacher. He, along with my daddy and Papa, never liked him.

I feel that I have a close relationship with God. I pray and I read my Bible and I know that He is with me. I also know it's times like these, when we have our doubts and hard times that we are supposed to have faith and trust Him. Those are the times when it is the hardest to do. I've been through a lot in my life but what happened to my brother shook me to the core and made me question everything that I believed. It made me wonder more than ever, why bad things have to happen to good people and why bad people get away with doing horrible things.

After I got home I felt impressed to send my mother a message that I thought may help her, when really I was probably the one who needed the help. She was being so strong. In that message I wrote that I didn't understand why things in life had to be this way. Why Donnie had to die this way. I didn't understand why a preacher stole my innocence when I was thirteen and took so many years from me.

I told her that if I could go back to when Donnie was a teenager and could stop him from trying the first drop of liquor and make a difference in his life and how things ended, I would take what I'd been through a hundred times over. I meant that with all my heart. If only life worked that way.

I was a victim of a preacher's manipulation, but I do think of how I was blessed to have good parents. I wasn't abused at home and I was always taken care of. Even going through what I went through with the Preacher, I was living in ignorant bliss and thought I was happy. I think of the children who have to live seven days a week in horrible homes. It is my life's promise that if I ever am in a child's life that I suspect is being abused in any way that I will do everything in my power to help them.

I've never sought professional help or gotten the opinions of experts who know about men like the Preacher. I suppose I've come to my own conclusion. That he is a sick, power hungry man, hungry for sex, women, and money. He loved to feed his ego with girls and women who he would trick into loving him. Because he did manipulate women into loving him, he thought and acted as though he were the greatest man that ever walked the earth. He was always very arrogant and I'm sure he still would be if he weren't out of his mind and wheelchair bound. You can't be too arrogant with your wife having to feed and bathe you.

While writing this book I recalled many past memories. So many I wish I could forget, especially now that I am older and wiser. But also many that I am glad that I have recalled because I believe that it has all helped in my recovery process. I remember in the beginning, before things went too far and the Preacher was only being a second grandpa to me. He would ask weird questions. He asked did my grandpa kiss me. I said that my Papa did kiss me on the cheek, and I would kiss him on his cheek. He would ask these strange questions about men in my life, my dad, grandpas, uncles, cousins. I didn't think a lot of it at the time.

Now I know that he was hoping that I had been abused in some way, maybe even honestly troubled. Maybe, to him, it would make doing what he did alright, because someone had already done it. Maybe that's how his brain worked. And maybe it was that he would have a dirty secret of mine to hold over my head. Maybe he tried to justify in his own sick mind the things he did. Even if I had been abused, that doesn't give him the right to do it. I wonder how many girls and women came and sought help from the Preacher because of abuse and he only saw that as a go for him to hurt them too.

He told me one day when he was taking another moment to remind me of my promise to him, and how important it was that I keep that promise. He would go to jail, his life would be over. And he said, "If you ever do tell, I will lie. I will lie and pull out every trick in the book!" None of this was really said in a threatening manner. Almost in a joking way, even. I just smiled at him and reassured him that he could trust me. I never dreamed I would tell. When it came down to coming forward to Pastor Bill and his wife, I HAD to tell. I had to tell or live the rest of my life in misery. I had to tell for me. It would be too much to live my life in misery, even for someone I loved. Today, I'm so glad I didn't keep a promise that never should have been asked of me to keep.

Had I been the only one that he manipulated, had I thought he really loved me, or his wife, then maybe I would hate myself for breaking my promise. If I still thought the way I did for many years, that he was a good man who made a mistake, I would feel bad. But when I spoke out and others came forward, the blinders were removed, and I could finally begin to heal and move forward. I know it all happened the way it was meant to happen, all in God's time.

The other woman who had been molested as a minor was brave enough to share her story with me, and I will be forever grateful to her. Had she not told me I never would have really, truly been able to move on with my life. Her story saved me. I was still to a point making excuses for the Preacher in a sense. I had people trying to convince me that he was a pedophile, but I still didn't see it that way. Now I do. Now I know that I was not the only child.

I do not regret for a second that I broke my promise to the Preacher. Because now I am sure that there were many others. I feel by me going forward I got a little bit of justice for them too. I am writing this book for all of us. It is now obvious that he used whoever he could, whenever he could, with whatever tactic suited that person best. I hope that he has enough of his mind left to think of us and to think of what he did to us every day.

I often wonder if the only reason he started a church was to be able to wield power over people. And in the process get women and an income for doing nothing. It is so clear today that once you are in a position of authority you can have just about anything. So many people (especially women) can fall into the trap of holding so much admiration for a man in a powerful position. Most times it's not even deserved.

Admiration is okay, but many times it can lead to more, especially when the person in authority initiates other things. And so many men know they can and will, even if it's wrong and can ruin lives. They cheat on good wives and break up families to feed their own selfish desires. I don't understand. And there are many men out there like the Preacher, more than most of us would like to believe. They can have all the women they want if the women are foolish enough to consent, but they can't and shouldn't have girls.

These men don't keep in mind that what is done in the dark always comes to light. It may take months and it may take years, but they will be found out. Unfortunately, the damage, by then has already been done. I believe the Preacher wasn't smart enough or didn't care enough to think his sins would be brought to the light. I am glad that I helped shine that light in his face.

The Preacher made fools of everyone in his life; he made a mockery of God and of Christianity. It is people and preachers like him that give God and Christianity a bad name. His deeds will not go unpunished. The Bible says, "Dearly beloved avenge not yourselves, but rather give place unto wrath: for it is written, Vengeance is mine; I will repay saith, the Lord." KJV Romans 12:19

God offers forgiveness, but we still reap what we sow. To be forgiven you have to show remorse and ask for it. None of us are perfect, but I believe that there is a special punishment for people like this man. Jesus said that there is a special punishment for those who abuse children. Mark 9:35 KJV.

I am fortunate to have come out of this still believing and trusting in God and knowing there was a reason. Many people are not that fortunate. Many people turn their backs on God. I can't help but wonder if it's their fault or the ones who caused it.

I can't comprehend how the minds of these men and women work. I don't understand how they justify to themselves doing these things and wreaking such havoc on the lives of others, especially children who don't know better and who trust them.

The only good thing that I have gotten out of this situation is, believing if this hadn't happened to me I may have been too trusting of people with my own children. Maybe I would have been naive about how bad the world can be. I have learned to keep my children safe and protect them at all costs. I am thankful for what could have been, but wasn't. I am blessed that with all the females the Preacher was with, that he didn't give me any diseases. God was keeping me safe from that.

I do realize that my life after the Preacher could have taken a much different path. I could have been attracted to and involved with the wrong men or I could have become like the Preacher: being sexually active with anyone I could and seeing it all as okay. Had I not met my husband when I did, it could have changed everything. I have learned in life that in a lot of cases it could always be worse. I have at times questioned my getting married and starting a family so young, but I know without a doubt that it was meant to be that way for my own good, even though it is not always easy.

I am also very thankful that in finally speaking out about what the Preacher had done to me I was able to really see that he never loved me and more importantly that I didn't really love him. Even many years after he was out of my life, I felt that he owned a piece of my heart. I finally got it back when I came to the realization that I was in love with someone who never really existed.

He was not who I thought he was in any way. I learned that even more by how he reacted when I came forward and when truths from others came out. After years and years he was finally unmasked, not only in front of me but in front of everyone around him.

I can't tell anyone that has had bad things happen, that you can totally forget, but you can be happy. It is not who you are, though it does have a small part in making you who you are. If it hasn't done anything except make you wiser about people and what they can be capable of, then it has served a great purpose.

The things that happen in life are learning and growing opportunities. We can learn from them or choose to be full of hatred and bitterness for the rest of our lives. Bitterness is not good for us or those around us. I have chosen not to be bitter and to do the best I can to live this life to the fullest and not let the past control me in any way.

I still have times that I think of what happened and wonder why it had to happen or what would be different if it hadn't happened to me. It comes in waves. I can go months and months and never recall the past, but then have a dream or a passing thought, and a lot comes back. At these times, I look to my children and my husband and am happy in that moment and how far we have come.

As long as I don't dwell on it, I only have a moment or two to remember who I am and how I want things to be. At these times, I also keep in the back of my mind the fact that that man has taken far too much of my life and far too many of my thoughts to be allowed to take any more of my happiness and contentment. I will not allow him to steal anything else from me or my family. Yes, I have scars. Scars never heal, sometimes they're always a visible reminder of the past, but scars do fade over time.

I know that my children don't deserve a mother who sits and sulks, or a mother who can't move forward and leave the past in the past or who uses substances to get through the days and nights. By God's grace, I have never been that mother and never will be. God has given me a purpose in life by giving me my children. And I strive to raise them to the best of my ability, and always be whatever they need me to be. I do hope that my protectiveness of my children is not too overbearing and that it works. I know and I hate that I can't protect them from everything.

My children are home-schooled, they go nowhere without me somewhere very close by. This is another effect of what the Preacher did to me. I hope that as my children get older that they understand why their mother is so nervous and afraid. I hope that I don't cause them any problems because of it. But I know firsthand what people are capable of. I don't ever want to risk their physical or emotional security.

I hope anyone reading this that has had something similar happen to them, who maybe have not moved on, will turn to God and see that He is the one who can bring you peace and comfort. If you don't have a family, lean on friends, or other loved ones. They have a way of giving us a purpose. If you don't have these, pray for them and God will give you the desires of your heart. Don't waste another minute on the one who hurt you or the bad memories that they have left with you. Don't let them continue to hurt you by letting them hinder your life in any way for any longer. I know sometimes it's easier said than done. I have to work hard not to let my past hauntings control me or my thoughts.

This world is a scary place. Our churches and schools can be scary places, but I don't want this book to discourage anyone from living, making friends, going to church, or sending their kids to school. I believe the key is not to lock ourselves or our children away, but to be involved in our children's lives and aware of what's going on in every aspect of our their lives and our own. Don't ever COMPLETELY trust anyone. Guard your children and yourselves. The bible tells us to put our trust in God and not in man.

Psalm 118:8 "It is better to trust in the Lord than to put confidence in man." I know from experience, man will let us down, but God never will. Even when things happen in this life that we don't understand, if we only believe, God is there with us to help us and to see us through. He will never leave us or forsake us.